EVER THE TWAIN

A COMEDY IN THREE ACTS

by

LENNOX ROBINSON

MACMILLAN AND CO., LIMITED
ST. MARTIN'S STREET, LONDON

1930

For permission to perform this play and for information as to the fee payable, application must be made to Messrs. Curtis Brown, 6 Henrietta Street, Covent Garden, London, W.C. 2.

EVER THE TWAIN
A Comedy in Three Acts

TO

DUDLEY DIGGES

WHO HELPED TO LAY THE FOUNDATIONS OF
OUR NATIONAL THEATRE AND WHO IS NOW
ONE OF AMERICA'S MOST DISTINGUISHED
ACTORS; AND TO

W. T. H. HOWE

OF CINCINNATI, OHIO; KINDEST OF
AMERICANS.

CHARACTERS IN THE ORDER OF THEIR APPEARANCE

CHESTERFIELD WRAGSDALE.

VIVIENNE WATERS.

EDWIN SALMON.

UDOLPHUS.

NICHOLAS BRICE.

MICHAEL LOVE.

MOLLY O'SULLIVAN.

MRS. GORDON A. BECK.

GORDON A. BECK.

BIRDIE CUMMINS.

CARL SVENSON.

FOUR NEGROES.

MANY LADIES.

HENRI.

ED.

ACT I.—The smoking-room of a trans-Atlantic liner.

ACT II.—A room in the house of the Gordon A. Becks, at Crampton, somewhere in the Middle West.

ACT III.—A private dining-room in a New York restaurant.

" East is east and west is west,
And never the twain shall meet."
RUDYARD KIPLING.

ACT I

*The scene is the first-class smoking-room on a small
trans-Atlantic liner.   There are small windows
all along one side and at the back, at the back
is also a door leading to the deck.   One
side is windowless, there is a fire-place on this
side in which an electric fire glows and, beyond
it, a door leads to the steward's pantry.
Through the windows during the act, at regular
intervals, passengers are seen passing, doing
" constitutionals."   The same people pass again
and again—two stout elderly women in conversation with each other, an old man, a young
German-looking man, occasionally perhaps a
sailor passes bent on business.   The time is
morning and the sea is calm though a slight
slow roll every now and then makes the horizon
line visible through the windows.   When the
curtain rises the room is empty, then*
CHESTERFIELD WRAGSDALE *and* VIVIENNE
WATERS *come in from the deck.*   WRAGSDALE
*is a prosperous sleek-looking Englishman about
forty-eight years old, he is dressed excellently
in an unobtrusive English way.* VIVIENNE
WATERS *is twenty-two, pretty in a rather conventional English-rosebud fashion, her manner*

9

is a little young and shy.   WRAGSDALE'S
manner is exceedingly assured.

WRAGSDALE. Not a soul here.   (*He tries the
door of the steward's pantry.*)   And the bar's still
locked.   I'm sorry.

VIVIENNE. It doesn't matter.   I don't want
anything.

WRAGSDALE. I confess I could do with a
spot.   I woke at three and I couldn't get to
sleep again with the racket those fellows made
pulling the baggage about.

VIVIENNE. I know.   Wasn't it awful?   And
the girl who shared my cabin was getting off at
Boston so she got up very early to finish her
packing.   Did your companion get off at Boston?

WRAGSDALE. My companion?

VIVIENNE. The man who shared your cabin.

WRAGSDALE. Oh, I've a single.   I never risk
a double cabin.   One doesn't know who one
might be thrown with.   Let's sit down.

(*They sit at a table.*)

VIVIENNE. The girl with me was quite nice
—of course she was an American.

WRAGSDALE. Exactly.   That's the kind of
risk one runs.

VIVIENNE. But she really *was* nice—for an
American.   I'll miss her.   Doesn't the ship
seem awfully lonely?   All the people one had
got to know have gone.

WRAGSDALE. Yes, the twenty-four hours

between Boston and New York are always rather ghastly, but you'll find today there will be a re-shuffle, you'll get to know people you've never seen before—like me.

VIVIENNE. Oh, I'd seen you before—not often, just a few times.

WRAGSDALE. I take it this is the first time you've crossed?

VIVIENNE. Yes. And you?

WRAGSDALE. My third. . . . Considering that we've talked together on deck for nearly an hour I think we might exchange names. Mine's Wragsdale—Chesterfield Wragsdale.

VIVIENNE (*wide-eyed*). What! Chesterfield Wragsdale! Someone said you were on board but your name wasn't in the passenger list.

WRAGSDALE. No, a stupid mistake of the purser's. I rated him for it.

VIVIENNE. When I thought you *were* on board I tried to place you. I thought you must be that young man with the nice hair, I never imagined . . .

WRAGSDALE (*conscious he is growing a little bald*). Which young man?

VIVIENNE. The one who is always looking after that girl who has been so ill and who lies out on deck all day and never comes down to meals. He sits beside her for hours and reads to her, poetry and beautiful things.

WRAGSDALE. You mean the fellow who wears the fantastic clothes?

VIVIENNE. Fantastic?

WRAGSDALE. Well, awful tweeds, awfully cut.

VIVIENNE. Are they? Yes, I suppose they are.

WRAGSDALE. And ghastly butcher-blue shirts.

VIVIENNE. Yes.

WRAGSDALE. Why, he's Irish, got on at Queenstown.

VIVIENNE. Did he?

WRAGSDALE. He's impossible. He was singing in here last night—singing!

VIVIENNE (*keenly*). Singing? What was he singing?

WRAGSDALE. I don't know. Irish songs, folk-songs I expect, to a lot of American men and they all got drunk, it was perfectly awful, I was playing bridge but I simply couldn't. I was so rattled I went three no-trumps on two queens and a jack bare.

VIVIENNE. I wish I'd heard him. I love folk-songs.

WRAGSDALE. You wouldn't have liked his. Fancy you taking him for me.

VIVIENNE. Yes, that was silly, wasn't it? Of course you couldn't be as young as that and have written all those wonderful novels.

WRAGSDALE. Oh . . . er . . . you've read some of my things?

VIVIENNE. Everything, I think. Every novel you've ever written. I simply adore them.

WRAGSDALE. Oh . . . er . . . I wonder which of them you like best.

VIVIENNE. The latest one I think—" The Light Beyond "—no, I think I like best of all " Moonlight in Babylon." What are you writing now—perhaps I shouldn't ask, I expect you hate talking about your work?

WRAGSDALE. No, I don't mind, and it's a question easily answered. I'm writing nothing.

VIVIENNE. What a shame! Why?

WRAGSDALE. I haven't time for any real work this winter, I'm booked for a ghastly lecture-tour.

VIVIENNE. Oh, how exciting.

WRAGSDALE. Not at all exciting. An awful bore, I hate it.

VIVIENNE. Then why do you do it?

WRAGSDALE. Oh, they insist, they positively insist.

VIVIENNE. They?

WRAGSDALE. My public.

VIVIENNE. The Americans who read your books?

WRAGSDALE. And who want to hear me talk. This is my third lecture tour.

VIVIENNE. What do you lecture on?

WRAGSDALE. The Future of the English Novel illustrated by Readings from My Own Works.

VIVIENNE. It must be wonderful, I'd love to hear you.

WRAGSDALE. Oh it's rather nonsense really but they like it—these women's clubs, these get-culture-quick groups.

VIVIENNE. I don't believe it is nonsense, and I suppose you make a lot of money.

WRAGSDALE. Not a lot—but I never think of the money side of it, I do it because—well because they do insist and because it's really rather touching, almost pitiful, this desire of theirs to get in touch, even for an evening, even for a single hour, with English civilization.

VIVIENNE. So I was right, it isn't just nonsense.

WRAGSDALE. No, I suppose it isn't, but I hate to seem to brag. I have something to give them, something they want very much and it would be churlish to refuse. You know when I go to a town for the first time I always make a point of visiting the public library and introducing myself to the library staff, they're ridiculously glad to meet a real live author, and if I visit the town again I let them know I'm coming and they arrange some awful tea and display one's books and the booksellers fill their windows with them and every second person at the tea-party has your last novel and it must be autographed—oh, what a nuisance it all is, what a waste of time.

VIVIENNE. Yes . . . but I think it's splendid of you to give up a whole winter to them when you might be writing a glorious novel.   I—I'm going out for much the same reason.

WRAGSDALE. You? Are you going to lecture?

VIVIENNE. Goodness no, I couldn't lecture. But I sing—old English songs and Scotch ballads—that's why I said I wished I had heard that Irishman sing.   I've always been afraid to try Irish songs, afraid of the brogue.

WRAGSDALE. I don't think Irish ballads are much good—certainly not the ones that fellow was singing last night.   The English ones are very jolly, aren't they?   " Widdicombe Fair " and things like that.   What is your name?

VIVIENNE. Vivienne Waters. I'm sure you've never heard of me, I'm only a beginner.   I sing in costume, and half my success, the little I've had, has been the dresses.   This American tour is a great chance for me.

WRAGSDALE. I'm sure it's a great chance for the Americans.   They love old English things. You should see how they prize what they call " colonial " things, colonial houses and colonial furniture, which really is only second - rate English eighteenth-century stuff.   You know in their hearts they'd give anything not to have broken away from England—of course you'll never get them to admit it.

VIVIENNE. Yes, poor things, what they've lost!   But you know the American girl who shared my cabin said " England was all right if you *wanted* a funeral."

WRAGSDALE. Poor girl! Inferiority complex. America is full of it. Whistling to keep their courage up. Really it's very pathetic.

(EDWIN SALMON *comes in. He is twenty-two, English. His speech has every fault of the uneducated English actor.*)

EDWIN (*trying the pantry door*). Good God, still shut. (*He presses a bell.*) Morning, Mr. Wragsdale.

WRAGSDALE. Good-morning.

EDWIN. Blighting sort of morning isn't it?

WRAGSDALE. How did you sleep?

EDWIN. I didn't. And nobody warned me about this limit business. I thought this was a British ship. What has Yankee prohibition got to do with us?

WRAGSDALE. We're still in American territorial waters.

EDWIN. You don't mean to say that the Americans own the sea?

WRAGSDALE. A little bit of it.

EDWIN. I say! I wish I'd known. Why didn't someone tell me? I'd have bought a bottle of Scotch last night.

WRAGSDALE. We'll be outside the limit any minute now, you won't have to wait long.

EDWIN. Thank God. Mind if I squat here?

WRAGSDALE. Not at all. May I—Mr. Salmon, Miss Waters.

VIVIENNE (*bowing*). How d'you do?

EDWIN. How d'you do. (*Sitting*) *Edwin*

16

Salmon is my name—there's another Salmon on the stage called Lionel or some quaint name like that and I hate people mixing me up with him. Isn't it perfectly devastating this morning, Miss Waters? I don't know why I didn't get off at Boston and take the train—there *is* a train I suppose from Boston to New York?—I don't believe I can exist on this awful ship for another day.

VIVIENNE. What's wrong with the ship?

EDWIN. What's wrong? What's right? It's so dashed slow, the food's so awful, it's crawling with Americans. I wish I'd waited a day longer and come by the *Mauretania*. Lots of my friends were coming over on her.

WRAGSDALE. I tried for a cabin on the *Majestic* but I was too late.

VIVIENNE (*simply*). I came on this boat because it's cheap. I couldn't afford those big boats.

EDWIN.
WRAGSDALE.
} Oh . . . ah . . . really?

(UDOLPHUS, *the smoking room steward comes in from the deck. He is English and speaks with a Lancashire accent.*)

EDWIN. Oh, Udolphus! Is it ever going to be possible in this world to get another drink?

UDOLPHUS. In about another three minutes, sir.

EDWIN. Well, take the order now and bring it to us the instant the old tub has staggered

across the line or passed the bally limit or whatever it is. What will you have, Miss Waters?

VIVIENNE. Just a ginger.

EDWIN. Oh, I say!

VIVIENNE. I'm afraid I never drink.

EDWIN. Really?

VIVIENNE Really.

EDWIN (*to* WRAGSDALE). And you?

WRAGSDALE. A small Scotch.

EDWIN. A dry ginger, two small Scotch and
a large soda, Udolphus.

UDOLPHUS. Yes, sir. (*He goes into his pantry.*)

VIVIENNE. Is his name really Udolphus?

EDWIN. Yes, *U*dolphus, not *A*dolphus.
Isn't it a scream?

> (NICHOLAS BRICE *comes in and settles himself
> at a table somewhat removed. He starts
> to play solitaire. He is an American of
> forty-five but looks older. He is very
> quiet in manner, his accent is only faintly
> American.*)

EDWIN. Of course, ghastly as this ship is, I'll
be sorry to leave it. It's dreadful to have to
nerve oneself to face America tomorrow.

VIVIENNE. I know. I'm simply terrified.

WRAGSDALE. There's really nothing to be
afraid of. You'll find Americans very kind,
primitive of course, sometimes a little uncouth,
but fundamentally kind . . . kind.

EDWIN. It's all right for you, old chap, you're
lecturing, you're on your own. But look at

me! I'll certainly be hated at first, quite naturally.

VIVIENNE. Why should anyone hate you?

WRAGSDALE. Mr. Edwin Salmon is going out to New York to join the caste of a new play.

VIVIENNE. Oh, how exciting!

EDWIN. It's not a bit exciting, it's rather a bore. And I don't like people not to like me. Childish of me, isn't it?

WRAGSDALE. You'll find they *will* like you, and like you a great deal. One of the touching things about them is their anxiety to learn. You can speak English properly, they can't and they know that they can't. You know they have a cigarette called " Pall Mall." Well, they call it " Poll Moll."

VIVIENNE. Not really?

EDWIN. How devastating!

WRAGSDALE. A fact, I assure you. Their treatment of the English language is un-believable. Tomahtoes, remember, are toma-toes.

EDWIN. Isn't it a scream?

VIVIENNE (*innocently*). But I wonder which is right. It's not an English word, is it?

WRAGSDALE (*crushingly*). Of course tomahto is right.

VIVIENNE. Yes, I suppose it is. . . . I wonder did I ever see you act. I saw most of the plays in London last summer.

EDWIN. Probably not. I confess I've been

idling lately, dreadfully slack of me, Ah, here, thank God, are the drinks.

(UDOLPHUS *brings them.*)

EDWIN (*giving him money and* UDOLPHUS *returning change*). Tomorrow I suppose we'll have to face that fantastic American money. Why do they have it?

WRAGSDALE. You'll have to make up your mind to it, they're not English.

EDWIN. I know. But doesn't it seem very silly? Thank you, Udolphus.

(UDOLPHUS *goes.*)

NICHOLAS (*to* UDOLPHUS *as he passes him*). A pale sherry, please.

UDOLPHUS. Yes, sir. (*During the following conversation, at a reasonable moment,* UDOLPHUS *brings* NICHOLAS *his sherry,* NICHOLAS *pays for it, no word is spoken.*)

EDWIN (*the soda in his hand*). How much?

WRAGSDALE. Half and half. . . . Thanks.

EDWIN (*having diluted his*). Well, here's to our success in the land of the free!

WRAGSDALE. Here's to your long run! (*He drinks.*) You know we're quite a little band of pioneers, we three, blazing, as it were, a trail through the American wilderness. Miss Waters is bringing them the beautiful folk-songs of the old country, you are going to let them hear English as she is spoke, and I shall talk to them about the English novel. We have each our different message.

VIVIENNE. I find it hard to believe that they want us—I mean that they want me.

WRAGSDALE. My dear young lady, they do, let me assure you that they do. They're hungering for us. But—an important point—don't sell yourself too cheap. They only appreciate what they pay for and the more they pay the more they appreciate.

VIVIENNE. Really?

EDWIN. They always think in terms of dollars, don't they?

WRAGSDALE. All the time. (*To* VIVIENNE) Who is your agent?

VIVIENNE. The Pollak Bureau.

WRAGSDALE. I've heard of it. Not very good, I'm afraid. My agent—Mr. Koffmann —is quite the best. He gets stiffer terms than anyone else.

VIVIENNE. Does he really?

EDWIN. Is living as beastly expensive as everyone says it is?

WRAGSDALE. It *is* expensive. Of course you get a lot of hospitality offered to you. I make a point of accepting it—though it's often a bore —because they so much appreciate your accepting it. They'll remember for years that you once stayed in their house. Touching, isn't it?

EDWIN. They won't be likely to offer to put up an actor, novelists are different. I believe they're getting me too cheap.

WRAGSDALE. I'm sure they are. We're all too cheap, really.

VIVIENNE. Surely *you*'re not cheap?

WRAGSDALE. I *have* lectured for four hundred dollars.

VIVIENNE. Four hundred! I'm only getting a hundred and fifty for my first recital, I don't know about the others. I thought it was a lot of money, but my travelling is paid, and if I travel at night I'm to have sleepers.

WRAGSDALE. The degrading promiscuity of the American sleeping-car!

VIVIENNE. What do you mean? Shall I have to sleep with a lot of other women?

WRAGSDALE. *And* men!

VIVIENNE. Not really? You're joking.

WRAGSDALE. I assure you the American sleeping-car is no joke. Do you like niggers?

VIVIENNE. I—I don't know.

WRAGSDALE. Your bed will be made by a nigger, you will be waked in the morning by a nigger. You will have to undress crouched on your bed, cramming your clothes into two small racks. It will be stiflingly hot, you cannot open a window. In the morning when you go to wash—well, I do not know what the ladies' arrangements are—I hope they are better than the men's, eight men trying to wash and shave in a space that might just accommodate two.

VIVIENNE. But how perfectly awful.

EDWIN. Tell me, how expensive are things?

WRAGSDALE. Take it all round, everything is three times as dear as in England.

VIVIENNE. ⎫
EDWIN.   ⎭ Three times!

WRAGSDALE. And therefore we've got to charge everyone five times as much as we would at home.

EDWIN. We've something to give that they haven't got.

WRAGSDALE. And they don't appreciate it unless we sell it dear.

EDWIN. The almighty dollar. They think of art in terms of that.

WRAGSDALE. Exactly.

(MICHAEL LOVE *and* MOLLY O'SULLIVAN *appear at the door.* MICHAEL *is a handsome young Irishman of about twenty-four,* MOLLY *is about twenty. She is countrified and shy, dressed in a new unbecoming black dress.*)

MICHAEL. It's all right; come on in.

MOLLY. Ah no, I won't.

MICHAEL. Can't you come on? It's too cold on deck, you'll get your death. Look, Mr. Brice is there.

MOLLY. Are you sure it's all right for me to come in?

MICHAEL. Of course. There's another girl there. (*She comes in a little unwillingly and they join* MR. BRICE *at his table. He rises courteously and greets them both.*)

23

VIVIENNE (*in a half voice*). There he is, the man I thought was you.

WRAGSDALE. I suppose I should be flattered, he's very good-looking.

EDWIN. He's really rather awful, I was forced to meet him a night or two ago. His name is Love, Michael Love.

VIVIENNE. What a perfect name.

EDWIN. Do you think so? Sounds like a movie star.

WRAGSDALE. And he looks a little like one. No, he's rather impossible, I can't forget last night's performance.

EDWIN. What did he do?

WRAGSDALE. Well he came into the smoking-room with a lot of Americans and—(*his voice drops, he proceeds in a whisper to tell the tale of last night's proceedings*).

NICHOLAS (*to* MOLLY). You're really feeling better this morning?

MOLLY. I'm feeling grand, thanks. At long last my stomach's got used to the sea.

MICHAEL. What'll you have, Molly?

MOLLY. I'd love a cup of tea.

MICHAEL. Udolphus couldn't give you tea at this hour—in the middle of the morning.

MOLLY. And why not? Sure any hour of the day is a good hour for tea.

MICHAEL. Udolphus !

VIVIENNE. I wonder who the girl is.

EDWIN. Irish, and terribly common. Look at her clothes, aren't they a scream?

VIVIENNE. And now please, Mr. Wragsdale, tell us more about this awful America. How much does a room in a moderate hotel cost?

EDWIN. Yes, how many dollars—— ?

> (*The three fall into an animated discussion for the next few minutes until* UDOLPHUS *visits them again. Nothing is heard from them but the words "dollars," "agents," "percentages," but these words are heard frequently.* UDOLPHUS *has come from his pantry to* MICHAEL.)

MICHAEL. A pale sherry, an Irish and—you must have something lively.

MOLLY. Well, a glass of wine.

MICHAEL. Port wine?

MOLLY. Please. If you're sure it won't make me sick.

MICHAEL. Of course it won't. A glass of port, Udolphus.

UDOLPHUS. A port, a pale sherry and a small Irish and soda.

MICHAEL. Pull yourself together, Udolphus. Water and a large Irish.

UDOLPHUS. Sorry, sir (*he disappears into the pantry*).

MICHAEL. She needs pulling together, Mr. Brice, she's terribly worried because she hasn't had a wire from her people in New York, she's afraid they won't meet her. You'll be all right,

Molly, sure if no one turns up I'll look after you, you won't be left walking the streets of New York all by yourself.

NICHOLAS. You're going to friends?

MOLLY. No, sir, to relations.

NICHOLAS. Oh well, that's all right.

MOLLY. To my sister-in-law, and I've never seen her in my life.

NICHOLAS. Can't your brother meet you?

MOLLY. No, sir.

MICHAEL. He can't, he's dead.

NICHOLAS. Oh. I'm so sorry.

MOLLY. It's terrible. And you see me a'nt didn't want the children to be brought up in New York, not after what had happened, she thought they'd get a better sort of education in Killeen, but of course she's handicapped with her bad leg and Julia said she couldn't be wasting her time dragging across the ocean——

MICHAEL. Julia's the sister-in-law——

MOLLY. So there was nothing for it but for me to come, but what'll I do if they don't meet me?

NICHOLAS. Haven't you their address? Don't you know where your sister-in-law lives?

MOLLY. Oh yes, sir, she lives in Brooklyn. That's a long way out I'm told.

MICHAEL. I'm telling you not to fret about it, Molly. I won't leave you till I land you on your sister-in-law's doorstep (UDOLPHUS *appears*). Good man, Udolphus. Score it up to me.

UDOLPHUS. Very well, sir (*he goes into his pantry*).

NICHOLAS (*drinking to* MOLLY). Here's luck to you, Miss O'Sullivan. And so you plan to take the children back to Ireland?

MOLLY. I do.

NICHOLAS. How many are there?

MOLLY. Two little boys. The eldest's eleven and the other's just pushing eight.

NICHOLAS. I see. Two little American boys.

MOLLY. Oh no, sir, they're Irish, sir. Their father and mother were both Irish. We couldn't leave them in New York, not after——

NICHOLAS. Not after what?

MOLLY. Ah nothing, sir.

MICHAEL. Her brother got into a bit of trouble, Mr. Brice.

MOLLY (*indignantly*). He did no such thing, Michael Love. Sure we all know what the police are, they're the same all the world over.

NICHOLAS. Oh, he got into trouble with the police?

MICHAEL. He was shot.

MOLLY. They murdered him Mr. Brice, they shot him dead. Wasn't that a fearful thing?

NICHOLAS. Dear, dear.

MOLLY. And they sailed away leaving him in gores of blood and of course not a word said against them.

MICHAEL. It's well known the New York police are hard characters.

NICHOLAS. Yes . . . they're mostly Irish. But how did it happen?

MOLLY. Jim had a little business—well indeed it wasn't so little for he did well out of it, used to send me a'nt home big money and send some to meself too. A kind of a restaurant he had and the police came in one night and they and Jim had a few words and they out with their guns and shot him dead.

NICHOLAS. A restaurant. . . . I see.

MOLLY. You'll have heard about it, of course.

NICHOLAS. As a matter of fact I hadn't. I haven't been in New York for quite a while.

MOLLY. I'm sure New York was ringing with it. So you see we couldn't leave the poor innocent little children to grow up with the shadow of that hanging over them.

NICHOLAS. New York forgets very quickly.

MOLLY. It couldn't forget a thing like that, not in twenty years.

NICHOLAS. And do you think your sister-in-law will let the children go?

MOLLY. Faith she must, I'll fight her for them tooth and nail. God knows, though, she's a hard woman. And I'm sure Jim left something to me a'nt in his will but ne'er a penny of it have we seen. I'll have to fight her for that too.

NICHOLAS. You've quite a lively time in front

of you, Miss O'Sullivan. No wonder you feel a trifle scared.

MOLLY. Oh, I'll get my rights, sure I've God on my side. But I can't help feeling a bit lonely today. I feel it'll be a terrible struggle to best Julia. Michael's been a good friend to me, Mr. Brice. I think I'd have died if it hadn't been for him. He made me eat and everything and he'd never clapped eyes on me till he saw me getting sick on the tender coming out from Cove. I wish to God, Michael, you were to be in New York.

MICHAEL. Ah, you'll do game-ball, never fear.

NICHOLAS. You're not stopping in New York?

MICHAEL. Only long enough to see Molly reaches her brother's place.

MOLLY. He's going the length and breadth of the States, Mr. Brice. Michael's a poet, a grand poet, and he's going lecturing and saying poetry through the four quarters of America.

NICHOLAS. I see. Another!

MICHAEL. Another what?

NICHOLAS. Nothing.

MICHAEL. I'm not much of a poet yet, but I've all the old songs and ballads of Ireland on the tip of my tongue. But your glass is empty, Mr. Brice. Udolphus!

NICHOLAS. Nothing more for me, I've had my allowance. Two sherrys before lunch.

MICHAEL. Nonsense. Sure what are two small sherrys ? (UDOLPHUS *appears*.) A sherry for Mr. Brice and you may as well bring me another whiskey—a small one this time.

NICHOLAS. No, really——

MICHAEL. I'll take no refusal, the last day before prohibition. You've got to drink success to Molly and confusion to Julia. You can't refuse.

NICHOLAS. Well——

MICHAEL. And, Udolphus, my compliments to Mr. Salmon and his friends and ask them what they'll have on me.

UDOLPHUS. Very well, sir (*he goes to the other table*).

NICHOLAS. I'm a lawyer, Miss O'Sullivan, if you are in any difficulty I might be able to help you. Will you take my card ?

MOLLY. Oh, sir !

MICHAEL. Take it, Molly, take it, and write down your name and address for him. I'm sure you can't have too many friends in New York and maybe he'll help you to best Julia.

MOLLY. Very well.

> (*She hasn't, of course, a card and there is a few minutes business of her writing her name and address on a slip of paper. Meanwhile* UDOLPHUS *has brought the discussion of dollars and percentages at the other table to an end.*)

UDOLPHUS (*to* EDWIN). Mr. Love's compliments, sir, and he wants to know what you and your friends would care to drink.

EDWIN. Oh, I say ! I really don't think—I hardly know the fellow.

WRAGSDALE. How extraordinary of him. It's not as if he had won the sweep on the day's run or anything like that.

VIVIENNE. I don't want anything to drink but I'd like to talk to him about folk-songs.

WRAGSDALE. I don't think from what I've seen of him that he's the sort of fellow you'd care to know.

EDWIN (*to* UDOLPHUS). Thank Mr. Love and say we're taking nothing more.

VIVIENNE. Thank him *very* much.

UDOLPHUS. Yes, miss (*he goes to the other table*). They say to thank you very much, sir, but they're taking nothing more.

MICHAEL. Oh, nonsense (*he gets up and comes over to them*). Good-morning, Mr. Salmon.

EDWIN. Good-morning.

MICHAEL (*to the whole table*). Look here, I've been making careful enquiries ; besides ourselves the first-class passengers from here to New York consist of five middle-aged ladies— the three knitters you know and the two old girls who keep themselves to themselves for you can *not* be too careful—the old man with the ear trumpet and the two Germans who speak no English. So we all may as well stick

together today and try and knock some fun out
of life. My name's Michael Love—Mr. Salmon
knows me—there's a nice little Irish girl over
there—come here, Molly—and the decentest
American I've ever met,—draw your chair
over, Mr. Brice. And what are you all
having?

WRAGSDALE. It's extremely kind of you, Mr.
Love, but really——

MICHAEL. I know you never take anything
so early in the day, etc., etc., all the same, give
it a name. Come over, Molly (*she comes, shyly*).
Now what is it to be?

WRAGSDALE. Well . . . er . . . I think a
Bronx.

VIVIENNE. I'll have the same.

WRAGSDALE. I thought you never——

VIVIENNE. I don't, but it's the last day, the
exception that proves the rule.

MICHAEL. That's the spirit. Mr. Salmon?

EDWIN. A small Scotch and soda.

MICHAEL. Got all that, Dolphy?

UDOLPHUS. Yes sir (*he goes to his pantry*).

MICHAEL. That's right, we won't bother
about introductions.

WRAGSDALE (*trying to regulate things*). My
name's Chesterfield Wragsdale, this is Miss
Vivienne Waters.

NICHOLAS (*politely*). How do you do?
Pleased to meet you, Miss Waters. Your
name, Mr. Wragsdale, is of course well known

to me though I confess I'm not much of a novel reader.

WRAGSDALE. Oh . . .ah . . . really?

MICHAEL. You look a bit peaky this morning, Salmon.

EDWIN. I feel a wreck, quite shattered. I had a devastating night. Didn't close an eye.

MICHAEL. I got drunk last night but I feel as fit as a fiddle this morning.

NICHOLAS. You're two of a trade you know, you ought to have met before. For Mr. Wragsdale —who is a very distinguished novelist—is I gather—I couldn't help a little overhearing your conversation—embarking on a lecture tour, and Mr. Love is also going to the States to lecture.

WRAGSDALE (*not very pleased*). Oh, really?

MICHAEL. Yes, I'm chasing the dollar. How many am I likely to overtake in three or four months ?

WRAGSDALE (*coldly*). I have no idea.

VIVIENNE. Mr. Wragsdale doesn't think of his lectures in terms of dollars.

MICHAEL. It's the only way I'm going to think of them.

NICHOLAS (*to* VIVIENNE). And you are going to sing old English songs to us—the American girl who shared your cabin told me that, and Mr.—er—Mr.——

EDWIN. Edwin Salmon is my name.

NICHOLAS. Mr. Salmon is a very distinguished English actor——

EDWIN. Oh come, draw it mild.

NICHOLAS. Well at any rate a young actor who is going to bring on the American stage, for a pleasant change, English in all its purity. I am the only American here.

WRAGSDALE. I should never have taken you for an American.

NICHOLAS. That, sir, I take it, coming from you, is a compliment.

WRAGSDALE. Not at all. I have a great admiration for the States, a wonderful country, a wonderful people, a great future——

NICHOLAS. When we have acquired a little culture?

WRAGSDALE. Er . . . yes. If you will forgive me.

NICHOLAS. There is nothing to forgive. No one is more aware of our uncouthness than myself. And it is natural for you to mistake me for a European, I spend a third of my year in Europe as a rule.

WRAGSDALE. What part of England were you in this summer?

NICHOLAS. I wasn't in England except for two business days in London before I sailed. Since July I've been in Tarragona.

VIVIENNE. Tarragona?

EDWIN. Never heard of it. Where is it?

NICHOLAS. Spain.

WRAGSDALE. You live in Tarragona?

NICHOLAS. Only for a few months in the summer, but I hope soon to be free of business and able to live there altogether.

WRAGSDALE. Do you ordinarily live in New York?

NICHOLAS. I have a bachelor apartment on Park Avenue and a country home on the Hudson.

WRAGSDALE. I shall be staying for a little while in New York. I'd very much like to look you up. May I?

NICHOLAS (*a little dryly*). I shall be honoured . . . I am fond of the theatre, Mr. Salmon, what play are you to appear in?

EDWIN. "Lady Betty," an English social comedy.

NICHOLAS. I see.

EDWIN. Do you think New York will understand English society life, won't it be a bit above their heads?

NICHOLAS. I don't think so.

EDWIN. I'm a bit nervous. But I do think it must be good for the American stage to have English actors, don't you?

NICHOLAS. I admire American acting, I think a great deal of it is very brilliant but I think that a great deal of American speech on the stage is deplorable. I am sure our players have much to learn from actors who have learnt to speak English beautifully, who come to us

35

with their Shakespeare at their fingers' ends,
their Sheridan, their Shaw. Where did you get
your training?

EDWIN. Oh I just knocked about—didn't go
to any of those awful Academies. I think the
stage itself is the best school.

NICHOLAS. I can quite believe it. Irving
. . . Tree . . . perhaps you were with the
Benson Company or are you too young?

EDWIN. 'Fraid I've never happened to be in
a Shakespeare play, the old boy doesn't draw
very well in England you know. My line is
light comedy.

NICHOLAS. Ah! (UDOLPHUS *arrives with the
drinks and hands them round.*)

MICHAEL. Chalk it up, Dolphy.

UDOLPHUS. Right, sir. (*He goes.*)

MICHAEL. Well, *slainthe!* (*He drinks.*) Mr.
Brice, you won't know your country in six
months' time, by the time we've done cultivating
you.

NICHOLAS (*drinking*). I hope you will all be
very successful and make a great deal of money
—even you, Mr. Wragsdale. And good luck
to you, Miss O'Sullivan, and may you "best"
—isn't that the word?—your sister-in-law.

MOLLY. Thank you, sir (*she sips her port*).

WRAGSDALE (*to* MICHAEL). Who is your agent?

MICHAEL. Agent?

WRAGSDALE. Who is arranging your tour?

MICHAEL. No one.

WRAGSDALE. No one? You're going out without an agent?

MICHAEL. Yes, I figured out I'd get on without one. I want to make money.

WRAGSDALE. I'm afraid you won't get very far without an agent. You won't get an engagement—at least I can't imagine that you will.

MICHAEL. I've an uncle in Boston, he's pretty high up in the police ; I've two sort of cousins in Chicago, one's a lawyer, his brother's a bootlegger ; I've a brother-in-law in St. Louis, an aunt in Baltimore well in with the Church— they're my agents.

WRAGSDALE. I see. . . . Why didn't you get off at Boston and go to your uncle?

MICHAEL. Ah, he's a bit of a free-thinker. I want to get my aunt busy first thing, if I get well in with the Church everything's O.K.   No, I'm going to keep off Uncle Mike for a while.

WRAGSDALE. I see. . . . Well!

NICHOLAS. I predict a most busy and profitable tour for you, young man.

MICHAEL. Oh, I think I'll do all right.

VIVIENNE. You sing, Mr. Love, don't you?

MICHAEL. No, not really. Just come-all-yes —old ballads you know.

VIVIENNE. I'd love to hear you.

MICHAEL. I've not much of a voice. Ask Mr. Wragsdale!

VIVIENNE. I sing old English ballads. Don't you love them?

MICHAEL. I'm afraid I don't know them.

VIVIENNE. They're very quaint.   I do them in costume.

MICHAEL. That must be grand.

MOLLY. I wish you'd sing one now, miss. I dote on music.

VIVIENNE. Oh, I couldn't sing here.

MICHAEL. Why not?   Sure we were all singing here last night.

EDWIN. It would be so jolly if you'd sing, Miss Waters, make us forget time passing and all that sort of thing.

VIVIENNE. No, no.

WRAGSDALE. I don't think she ought to——in the smoking-room.

MICHAEL. Haven't I told you that there are no able-bodied passengers on the ship barring ourselves?   Look here, Miss Waters, if I sing will you sing afterwards?

NICHOLAS. That's a fair bargain.

WRAGSDALE. But really——what will people think, at this hour of the day——?

MICHAEL. Sure let them think what they like and be——.   Aren't you a guarantee of our respectability?   Please!

VIVIENNE. I believe I will, though I can see Mr. Wragsdale doesn't approve.   That's the result of my having a cocktail.   But Mr. Love must sing first.

MICHAEL. Surely.   But remember I'm no prima donna.   This is only to break the ice.

(Without any self-consciousness he sits back in his chair, his glass in his hand and sings " The Maid of the Sweet Brown Knowe.")

Come all ye lads and lassies and listen to me a
    while,
And I'll sing for you a verse or two will cause
    you all to smile;
It's all about a young man, and I'm going to
    tell you now
How he lately came a-courting of the Maid of
    the Sweet Brown Knowe.

Said he " My pretty fair maid, if you and I agree,
We'll both go off together and married we will
    be;
We'll join our hands in wedlock bands, I'm
    speaking to you now,
And I'll do my best endeavour for the Maid of
    the Sweet Brown Knowe."

This fair and fickle young thing, she knew not
    what to say,
Her eyes did shine like silver bright and merrily
    did play;
She said " Young man, your love subdue, for I
    am not ready now,
And I'll spend another season at the foot of the
    Sweet Brown Knowe."

Said he, " My pretty fair maid, how can you
    say so?

Look down in yonder valley where my crops do
    gently grow,
Look down in yonder valley where my horses
    and my plough
Are at their daily labour for the Maid of the
    Sweet Brown Knowe."

" If they're at their daily labour, kind sir, it's
    not for me
For I've heard of your behaviour, I have, in-
    deed," said she;
" There is an inn where you call in, I have
    heard the people say,
Where you rap and you call and you pay for
    all, and go home at the break of day."

" Well, if I rap and I call and I pay for all, the
    money is all my own.
And I'll never spend your fortune, for I hear
    you have got none,
You thought you had my poor heart broke in
    talking with me now,
But I'll leave you where I found you, at the
    foot of the Sweet Brown Knowe."

NICHOLAS. Excellent, excellent.

MOLLY. Well done, Michael.

EDWIN. What a quaint song.

VIVIENNE. I must get the music. Another,
please.

MICHAEL. No, now it's your turn.

VIVIENNE. I think Mr. Salmon should do something first.

EDWIN. Quite impossible I'm afraid, I don't sing at all.

MICHAEL. Well, give us a recitation. I never knew an actor yet that couldn't recite.

EDWIN. A recitation? Good God, no, they're dreadful things.

MICHAEL. I love them. "The Green Eye of the Little Yellow God," or "The Dream of Eugene Aram," or "Mandalay."

EDWIN. Nothing doing, old man.

WRAGSDALE. I think there is something to be said for recitations. There are certain noble passages—Shakespeare, for instance.

MICHAEL. Come on, give us one.

WRAGSDALE. Shall I? Really? You'll have to be lenient, I'm not a professional entertainer, I have no parlour tricks. But this I happen to be very fond of :

" This royal throne of kings, this scepter'd isle,
This earth of majesty, this seat of Mars,
This other Eden, demi-paradise,
This—er—this——

MICHAEL (*prompting him sotto-voce very rapidly*).
" This fortress built by Nature for herself."

WRAGSDALE.
" This fortress built by Nature for herself
Against infection and—and the hand of
war,
This happy breed of men, this little world,

41

This precious stone—this—this precious
    stone—

MICHAEL (*finishing it with a flourish*).

" This precious stone set in a silver sea,
    This blessed plot, this earth, this realm, this
                                England."

VIVIENNE. Beautiful, Mr. Wragsdale, quite
beautiful.

EDWIN. Jolly good, I call it.   Jolly good.

WRAGSDALE. Thanks to Mr. Love.   I am
surprised at an Irishman knowing that passage.

MICHAEL. Oh the Christian Brothers bet
that into me.   Now, Miss Waters, no more
shirking.

VIVIENNE. I suppose I must keep my
promise.   But I'll have to stand up.   (*She gets
up, moves outside the table.*)   You must imagine a
very pretty, eighteenth-century dress, flowered
muslin or brocade, high hair.   As I told
Mr. Wragsdale the dress is half the battle.
And a harpsichord or a spinet.

> (*She sings an eighteenth-century song.   She
> has not a big voice, but it is well-trained,
> and she sings with a great deal of
> charm.*)

MOLLY. Isn't it lovely, Michael?

MICHAEL. It's great.

WRAGSDALE. Delightful, Miss Waters.   There
are no songs like the old English ones.

MICHAEL. Now it's America's turn.   Mr.
Brice!

NICHOLAS. America's contribution must, I fear, be silence.

MICHAEL. Nonsense.

NICHOLAS. A fact. I can't sing, I can't even recite.

MICHAEL. Can't you give us your national anthem—" The Star-spangled Banner " or whatever it is? I want to know it, I want to know when to stand up.

NICHOLAS. Impossible.

VIVIENNE. Or one of those wonderful Negro spirituals?

NICHOLAS. Certainly not. I intensely dislike this modern craze for the Negro. You'll have to skip me.

MICHAEL. Then the next item on the programme, ladies and gentlemen, is a song by Udolphus.

> (UDOLPHUS *since the beginning of the first song has been hovering in the background, eagerly listening. At this attack on him, he dives for his pantry.*)

UDOLPHUS (*disappearing*). No, no, sir.

EDWIN. Udolphus?

WRAGSDALE. The steward? Well, really!

MICHAEL (*getting up*). He's great, he was singing for us last night, after you had all gone to bed. (*He pursues* UDOLPHUS, *captures him and leads him back.*) Come along, Dolphy, there's no use your saying you can't, I've not forgotten last night, drunk as

I was. Only not those songs, there are ladies present.

UDOLPHUS. I couldn't really, sir.

MICHAEL. Yes, you can.

UDOLPHUS. I'd get into trouble.

MICHAEL. Not you.

WRAGSDALE. He really might, you know.

MICHAEL. Not at all. He can stand with his back to the door. If the captain comes in I'll swear it was me who was singing. Come on. Dolphy, be a sport. If you don't, it's the last drink you'll ever have on me.

MOLLY. Please, Mr. Udolphus.

VIVIENNE. Yes, please.

UDOLPHUS. Very well, Mr. Love, very well, ladies and gentlemen. Just a verse. (*He looks furtively at the door and sings with gathering confidence*).

> " It was on a Tuesday evening
>   At the home of Madge Malone,
>   There was quite a celebration
>   For the old man wasn't home.
>   There were songs and witty stories
>   And a bottle on the shelf,
>   When up sprang Dan McGrew and said
>   ' Here's a song I wrote myself.'

MICHAEL (*singing*). Sing it, Dan, go on.

UDOLPHUS.

> " She was just a sailor's sweetheart,
>   And she loved a sailor lad,

But he left her broke in Hertford,
He was all she ever had,

MICHAEL (*singing*). ("Except a dozen children").

UDOLPHUS.

"She still believes in sailors
And is true to the Red White and Blue,
And although she's barred
From the navy yard
She loves her sailor man posit*iv*ely."

That's all I remember of it. (*He escapes to his pantry*).

MICHAEL (*shouting after him*). Why don't you go on the halls, Udolphus?

WRAGSDALE. There's nothing, after all, like the English music-hall song of twenty years ago.

EDWIN. They're so quaint and archaic, aren't they?

NICHOLAS. And all this time here's Miss O'Sullivan sitting as quiet as a little mouse, yet I'm sure she knows many a good Irish song.

MICHAEL. Yes, Molly, it's your turn.

MOLLY. Me sing? I couldn't, Michael, you know well I couldn't.

MICHAEL. I know nothing of the kind.

VIVIENNE. Do please. I want so much to hear some more Irish songs.

WRAGSDALE. Yes, please.

EDWIN. It would be quite delightful if you would.

MOLLY. But I can't sing.

MICHAEL. I can't but I did. Look, Molly, there's been two English songs and a recitation to one Irish song. That's not fair. More injustice to Ireland. You must sing.

NICHOLAS. Please, Miss O'Sullivan.

VIVIENNE. Yes, please.

MOLLY. Very well so. But I've only a little bit of a voice. I hoped one time I'd be a great singer but the nuns told me to put that idea out of my head.

> (*She stands up in her seat, folds her hands in front of her like a school-girl reciting and sings very simply and charmingly.*)

" I know where I'm going,
I know who's going with me,
I know who I love,
But the dear knows who I'll marry.

I'll have stockings of silk,
Shoes of fine green leather,
Combs to buckle my hair,
And a ring for every finger.

Feather beds are soft,
And painted rooms are bonny ;
But I would leave them all
To go with my love Johnny.

Some say he's dark,
But I say he's bonny,
He's the flower of them all,
My handsome, coaxing Johnny.

> I know where I'm going,
> I know who's going with me,
> I know who I love,
> But the dear knows who I'll marry."

You would make me do it, Michael. (*She sits down quickly overcome with self-consciousness.*)

MICHAEL. Sure it was all right.

NICHOLAS (*particularly struck*). Charming, charming.

> (*The bugle for luncheon sounds. The three English rise instantly like a flock of birds.*)

WRAGSDALE.
VIVIENNE.   } That's lunch.
EDWIN.

(*The three go out*).

MICHAEL (*looking after them*). They certainly love their food. (BRICE *rises*.) Are you off too, Mr. Brice ?

NICHOLAS. I like a little turn on deck before luncheon, I'll see you both later.

(*He goes out.*)

MOLLY. She's very pretty, isn't she ? I wish I could sing like that.

MICHAEL. Oh she's not bad.

MOLLY. I feel terribly stupid ; you're all going out singing or lecturing or something, and I'm doing nothing at all.

MICHAEL. I should think fighting Julia was the hardest job of all.

MOLLY. 'Deed I suppose it is. Half the

time I see myself sailing home with my tail between my legs and no children at all.

MICHAEL. Ah nonsense. And Mr. Brice will be a good friend for you to have. Don't go and lose his card now.

MOLLY. I won't. But I'd be afraid to ask him for anything.

MICHAEL. You'll have to get over your fears. He'll be delighted to help you, he likes you, that's easily seen.

MOLLY. Sure how could he like me and he only speaking to me for a minute yesterday and for five minutes just now ?

MICHAEL. Oh those old fellows who have knocked about are very quick with their likes and dislikes. As long as he doesn't like you too much ! For God's sake, Molly, don't go and marry a Yank.

MOLLY. There's not much fear of that. Talk sense.

MICHAEL. I'd hate to think of you stopping in the States.

MOLLY. Sure I'm only out to go back with the children. When will you be going back yourself ?

MICHAEL. In time for Christmas, please God.

MOLLY. I bet you'll stay for good and all.

MICHAEL. Not me. I'm only out to make a bit of money for my father, he's on the edge of bankruptcy. If I can gather two hundred and fifty pounds then he's clear and I sail away home.

That's only twelve hundred dollars, maybe I'd make them in a couple of months, maybe I'd get back by the end of November.

MOLLY. I'll be home before you anyway.

MICHAEL. Will you meet me at Cove ?

MOLLY. I will.

MICHAEL. I'll spend a day and a night in Cork before I go home. God, I'll be praying prayers to be back.

MOLLY. If Cork was where New York is now, and we sailing to it——

MICHAEL. And I with two hundred and fifty nice pounds saved——

MOLLY. And I with the children——

MICHAEL. We'd be game-ball, Molly, wouldn't we ?

MOLLY. We would.

MICHAEL. But we're not game-ball yet.

MOLLY. We will be, with the help of God.

MICHAEL. Your hand on it, Molly O'Sullivan.   (*They clasp hands.*)

MICHAEL (*singing, half-mockingly*).
  "I know where I'm going,
  I know who's going with me,
  I know who I love,

MOLLY (*singing*).
  "But the dear knows who you'll marry."

CURTAIN

ACT II

The time is about three months later. The scene is the small mid-west city of Crampton in the home of MR. *and* MRS. GORDON A. BECK. *We see a curious room the width of the stage but very narrow. The stage falls into two distinct parts. Looking at it, as member of the audience, the left half of the stage is like the interior of an old English dwelling-house. The corner is filled by a great hooded fireplace placed diagonally across it, a wood fire burns on the great hearth, there are old iron fire-dogs, above on the high mantel-shelf is old pewter. Along the left wall stretches a great oak dresser, partly filled with pewter plates and old English china, partly with books very neatly arranged ; where there is space on the walls it is filled with coloured sporting prints or examples of Lovat Fraser's work. In front of the fire are a gate-legged table and a couple of uncomfortable Elizabethan chairs, and near the fire, on the back wall, is a high-backed black oak settle. This distinctly " old-English " scene stops abruptly half-way across the stage, the back wall becomes a modern wall tastefully panelled and devoid of pictures. The only furniture on*

*the right side of the stage is a small modern
table, covered with a coloured linen cloth.   In
the middle of the right side wall is an opening into another room, the opening is draped
with curtains American-fashion.   As the stage-
curtain rises* VIVIENNE WATERS *is heard singing, evidently from behind the panelled wall;
she is singing one of her typical old English
songs.   It is heard distinctly, but not loud
enough to drown conversation on the stage.
Thirty seconds after the curtain rises* MRS.
GORDON A. BECK *comes through the door on the
right; she has a tray in her hand, on which are
half a dozen cups and saucers.   She is a large
middle-aged woman with close-cropped grey
hair and rimless glasses.   The time is evening
and the room is brightly lit.   As she is arranging the cups on the modern table a bell is heard
to ring in the distance.*

MRS. BECK (*calling softly*). Gordon ! . . .
Gordon !

> (GORDON BECK, *her husband, puts his head
> in from the right.   He is about the same
> age as his wife, but whereas she is a large
> woman he is a tiny man.   At the moment
> he is enveloped in large coloured overalls.
> He has a can of peaches in his hand which
> he is trying to open.*)

GORDON. Dearest ?

MRS. BECK. The door. . . .   Birdie Cummins.

51

GORDON. These blamed peaches——

MRS. BECK. Ssh! Give them here. (*She takes them.*) Run and open the door. (*He is going.*) Better take off your overalls, it mightn't be Birdie.

> (*He goes, struggling to extract himself from the overalls as he disappears.* MRS. BECK *succeeds in opening the peaches, she brings them into the room on the right, then she comes back. All this time* VIVIENNE'S *song continues. An instant after* MRS. BECK *comes back* BIRDIE CUMMINS, *a pretty girl of twenty, comes in followed by* GORDON.)

GORDON. It *was* Birdie. (*He starts to get into the overalls.*)

MRS. BECK (*kissing her*). Birdie Cummins, you're just too good.

BIRDIE. Not at all, Mrs. Beck, but I'm sorry I'm late. After school I had to go across to Philipsburg and only got your message half an hour ago, then I found I was out of gas——

MRS. BECK. It doesn't matter, you're here anyway. I'm simply distracted, I don't know where to turn—oh, Gordon, don't stand teetering around, do something.

GORDON (*in difficulties*). These overalls——

MRS. BECK. Help him, Birdie.

BIRDIE. Let me, Mr. Beck. (*She helps him.*)

GORDON. Seems I can't get the blamed things right, Norah's so wide——

MRS. BECK (*after he has been girded*). Now, darling, there's no time to lose.

GORDON. Where's my peaches gone to?

MRS. BECK (*indicating the right-hand door*). In there, I opened them. (*He is going.*) The *glass* dish, darling.

GORDON (*disappearing*). Of course, dearest.

BIRDIE. What's happened anyway?

MRS. BECK (*tragically*). Norah's gone!

BIRDIE. Gone?

MRS. BECK. Walked out at six o'clock.

BIRDIE. Oh, for heaven's sake, why?

MRS. BECK. The quartet from the Baptist Church. She got real sore and said she " wasn't hired to wait on a bunch of damn Negroes."

BIRDIE. And she a Negro herself. Well, Mrs. Beck, I knew you were going to get yourself into trouble when you invited those Negroes along.

MRS. BECK. I'm getting myself into no trouble, Birdie Cummins. When I met Miss Waters in Chicago last month and fixed with her to come here tonight I promised her Negro spirituals. I'd never have got her if I hadn't. My little Circle can't afford big fees but I told her we had one of the loveliest Negro choirs and——

BIRDIE. I know, but you sure are in for trouble.

MRS. BECK. I don't believe I am. Everyone's here except the Churchills and Miss Sims and old Mrs. Whooley and I believe she genuinely has got grippe—— (*raising her voice*) the sandwiches, Gordon. The De La Huntys are here and the Regans—if only Norah hadn't beat it.

BIRDIE. But, say, what's the idea of eating in here? That little table won't accommodate sixty women.

MRS. BECK. I'll tell you as we go along. Help me set the table. I just want to be able to serve six or eight people here very quietly.

BIRDIE (*parking her coat and hat on a chair*). I thought it was only a Negro *quartet*.

MRS. BECK. Oh, it's not the Negroes, of course we won't feed *them*, that's what I explained to Norah—— (*Gordon appears with two plates of sandwiches.*)

GORDON. The sandwiches, darling.

MRS. BECK (*patiently but reproachfully*). Not those, dearest, the special ones on the little table. I told you.

GORDON. Sorry, darling. (*He disappears.*)

MRS. BECK. Throw a stick on the fire, Birdie.

BIRDIE. How's the talk going?

MRS. BECK. Splendidly, dear. She's just finished a song. (*She goes to the panelled wall and puts her ear to it.*) Yeah, she's talking. She's sweet, her agents were surely right when they billed her as the Wild Rose of Old England. No, the food's not for the Negroes, it's Chesterfield Wragsdale, he's coming.

BIRDIE (*dropping a stick*).   What?

MRS. BECK (*with immense satisfaction*).   Yeah.
I got him.

BIRDIE. Well, Mrs. Beck, I've got to hand
it to you.

MRS. BECK. I went to his lecture this afternoon, it was packed, I could hardly get in.   I
went around behind afterwards and found he
was stopping in town overnight, so I asked him
up here, at first he didn't want to come but I
just pestered him till he finally gave in.

BIRDIE. That's swell, I'm crazy to hear him.

MRS. BECK. Oh, he's not going to speak, I
had to promise that he wouldn't be asked to
speak and that he wouldn't have to meet all the
Circle.   He's to be shown right in here and
meet just a few of the nicest people.   (*Calling.*)
Gordon!

BIRDIE. I was kicking myself all over for
not being able to hear him this afternoon.
You're a marvel, Mrs. Beck.

MRS. BECK. Well honestly, Birdie, I don't
think I'd have got him tonight only that he
crossed on the same boat as Miss Waters and
wants to meet her again.   But, come to think
of it, Birdie Cummins, why did you tell me you
wouldn't come tonight?   Surely you're broad-
minded enough not to have anything against
coloured people.

BIRDIE. No, it wasn't the Negroes.   But I
had a date with Carl, made it before I remem-

bered it was Circle night and as I've failed him twice running I didn't dare put him off again.

MRS. BECK. Well to think you'd miss Vivienne Waters for Carl Svenson! Why she's one of the most perfect artistes that's ever been this side. The luck of getting her to a little place like Crampton! . . . (*Gordon appears with plates of sandwiches.*) Thanks, darling, those are right. (*The ladies take the plates from him.*) Just go on setting out the cups. (*He disappears.*) Try one of these, they're Norah's speciality, thank goodness she had made them before she knew about the Negroes. (*A sound of music is heard.*) She's singing again. Sit down, if we keep still we'll hear almost as well as if we were in the room with her.

BIRDIE. Isn't there anything you want done?

MRS. BECK. Practically everything's fixed, Gordon can finish. (*Raising her voice.*) Gordon! There's a box of napkins.

GORDON'S VOICE. Of course, dearest.

MRS. BECK (*sitting*). I'm all worn out, but a little music will rest me. (*She starts on a sandwich.*) Delicious!

BIRDIE (*taking her second sandwich*). Yeah, aren't they? I always said that Norah's sandwiches——

MRS. BECK (*with dignity*). I meant the music.

BIRDIE. Of course it's lovely.

MRS. BECK (*joining in somewhat uncertain as to words and air*). "Hey nonny no, hey nonny

56

no." . . . Delightfully English. . . . Oh,
Mr. Beck *can* manage it.

BIRDIE. It?

MRS. BECK. The trip this summer. We'll
leave first week in June and needn't be back till
September.

BIRDIE. How perfectly lovely.

MRS. BECK. And you'll come too.

BIRDIE. I wish I could.

MRS. BECK. Of course you can. I'll speak
to your mother tomorrow.

BIRDIE. I guess Europe can't see me this
summer.

MRS. BECK. Now, Birdie Cummins, you've
got to. You remember how you enjoyed that
English trip last summer and this will be Italy,
Genoa and Torino and Sienna and Fierenze and
all sorts of wonderful little quartro-cento places,
and all the pictures—you know you're crazy
about pictures—old masters everywhere, Titian
and Pergolese and Canaletto and Sierra and
Guardi and Fra Angelico Kauffman.

BIRDIE. It sounds just wonderful, but I
don't believe I can.

MRS. BECK. You're not going to sit there and
tell me it's that Carl?

BIRDIE. Of course not.

MRS. BECK. He's a steady boy, but so crude,
darling, you must see yourself that he's terribly
crude.

BIRDIE. Sure, Carl's a bit crude.

MRS. BECK. And so young, and hardly a cent.

BIRDIE. Yeah.

MRS. BECK. And all his people are so crude —Swedes! (*Raising her voice.*) Gordon! I'm glad you agree with me, Birdie.

BIRDIE. All the same I like Carl quite a bit.

MRS. BECK. Of course, we all do. If he'd only get a mite cultured.

GORDON (*appearing*). Yes, darling?

MRS. BECK. I think Birdie could do with a fruit cocktail.

BIRDIE. Oh no, really, Mrs. Beck——

MRS. BECK. There are plenty. One for me too, Gordon. But hurry. (*Gordon disappears.*) Chesterfield Wragsdale's coming the minute he's through dinner at the hotel.

BIRDIE. Didn't the Swaffers put him up?

MRS. BECK. No, though he wrote saying he loved seeing real American homes, Mabel Swaffer showed me the letter.

BIRDIE. The Swaffers are just so mean.

MRS. BECK. I know, but Mabel Swaffer says that if the Art Union gives a lecturer all those hundreds of dollars he can afford a hotel. I believe the fact is Ned Swaffer gets mad if Mabel brings artists around the house. Ned hasn't a scrap of artistic temperament.

BIRDIE. It would he such a privilege to have Chesterfield Wragsdale stop with you.

MRS. BECK. I know. I'm so pleased to have

Miss Waters stop here. (*Gordon appears with two fruit cocktails.*) Thanks, darling. (*Gordon goes.*)

BIRDIE. What was Mabel Swaffer wearing this afternoon?

MRS. BECK. I declare I didn't notice, it's queer about Mabel, spite of all her dollars and Ned's position she fades out, you just never notice her. (*A ring is heard.*)

MRS. BECK (*jumping up*). There he is, there he is. Gordon!

GORDON'S VOICE. Dearest?

MRS. BECK. The bell, darling, the bell. Quick!

GORDON'S VOICE. Yes, darling.

MRS. BECK (*at her vanity bag, polishing*). I look terrible.

BIRDIE (*also polishing*). So do I.

MRS. BECK (*suddenly screaming*). Gordon!

GORDON'S VOICE (*far away*). Dearest?

MRS. BECK. Your overalls.

GORDON'S VOICE. They're off.

MRS. BECK. Miss Waters is due to go on for another quarter of an hour at least, won't it be lovely to have a little quiet talk with him all to ourselves ?

BIRDIE (*tidying away her coat and hat and putting her vanity bag on the dresser where it gets hidden*). What was the name of his last book?

MRS. BECK. "Small Souls," wasn't it?

BIRDIE. No, that's Couperus.

MRS. BECK. It was small something. What was the one before it?

BIRDIE. " The Gold Spoon."

MRS. BECK. That's Galsworthy.

BIRDIE. Is it? It's awful not to remember. Can you remember the name of a single one?

MRS. BECK. No.

BIRDIE. And you were at his talk this afternoon. Didn't he mention any of them ?

MRS. BECK. Yeah he did, but I can't remember. I'll start by asking him which he likes best himself, that'll give us one name anyway. Ssh! Here he is. (*She stiffens, becomes the hostess.*) Ah, Mr.—— (*She suddenly relaxes.*) Why, Carl!

(CARL SVENSON, *a stocky young man of twenty-three comes in.*)

CARL. Hello, Mrs. Beck.

MRS. BECK (*a little coldly*). Good-evening, Carl. Who'd ever think of seeing you here tonight?

CARL. What's the matter with my coming tonight?

MRS. BECK. It's my Circle night.

CARL. I know, don't be scared, I won't butt in. Just come round from Birdie's place. We were going dancing tonight.

BIRDIE. I didn't forget, Carl, but when I got in there was an S.O.S. from Mrs. Beck and I came right on here.

CARL. What's the big idea?

MRS. BECK.
BIRDIE. } Chesterfield Wragsdale is coming!

CARL. Who the heck's he?

MRS. BECK. Carl Svenson!

BIRDIE. Don't mind him, Mrs. Beck, I'll bet Carl knows more about him than either of us do, he's just acting the boob.

MRS. BECK. Maybe you know the name of his last book. Do you, Carl?

CARL. "The Light Beyond."

MRS. BECK. Of course. Dumb of me to forget—he read a piece from it this afternoon.

BIRDIE. He's coming here unexpectedly, Carl, and Norah's beat it because there's Negroes coming.

CARL (*looking through the door*). Gosh, look at Gordon all dolled out in Norah's overalls. Say, can I help, Mrs. Beck, cut pie or something?

MRS. BECK. There's no pie.

CARL. 'Scuse. Forgot it wasn't an orphan's outing.

MRS. BECK. There's nothing you can do, Carl, thank you very much. I'm sorry for taking Birdie from her dance but she can go dancing any night and she may never get the opportunity of Chesterfield Wragsdale again. I won't press you to stay now, I know you don't appreciate my Circle.

CARL (*listening*). Ssh! that's nice. Who's singing?

MRS. BECK. Vivienne Waters.

CARL. Who's she?

MRS. BECK. Old English.

CARL. Oh hell!

MRS. BECK. Carl Svenson!

CARL. Sorry, Mrs. Beck, that just slipped out. My subconscious, you know. But I'm not going ; I'd figured out to have this evening with Birdie and if I can't have it dancing I'll have it at the circus—I mean the Circle.

MRS. BECK. Well, Carl, you must behave.

CARL. Sure, Mrs. Beck, I'll behave.

MRS. BECK. I mean behave well.

CARL. And I mean behave well. I'll behave so pretty that you won't believe it. Can't I behave pretty, Birdie?

(*There is a crash of breaking china.*)

CARL.   ⎱ Gee, cripe !
MRS. BECK. ⎰ Gordon !

GORDON'S VOICE. Only a bunch of plates, darling.

MRS. BECK. Oh Gordon, Gordon!

(*She hurries out,* BIRDIE *is following, but* CARL *stops her.*)

CARL. Let her be, it's only a few dishes. (*She goes back to the fire.*) You're a nice one, throwing a feller over like this. If I hadn't such a lovely nature I'd have given you the air.

BIRDIE. She sent a desperate message, you'd think something awful had happened, I just had to come, but we've done nothing since

I came except sit around and eat sandwiches. Try them, they're good. (*She starts on her fruit cocktail.*)

CARL. Thanks. (*He takes a sandwich and swallows it at one gulp.*) Norah sure makes good sandwiches.

BIRDIE. These are better. (*She offers another plate; they both sample them and absentmindedly continue eating until the end of the scene.*)

CARL. Say, I've got something I want to say to you. Can't you get away?

BIRDIE. I've got to help Mrs. Beck through. In half an hour there'll be sixty women to be fed. What's on your mind anyway?

CARL. My uncle's given me the farm?

BIRDIE. I don't get you. . . . Oh, you mean the one you were trying to rent from him?

CARL. Yeah. He said he was willing it to me anyway, he's seventy and reckoned he might live for twenty years more and be less and less able to look after it and I'd be getting older and older, so he's coming to live in his house in Crampton and I'll go out to his farm.

BIRDIE. But what about your own farm?

CARL. I'll keep it on. Five years with luck and I'm a rich man.

BIRDIE. I'm glad, Carl. Only I suppose we'll not see much of you now, you'll be so far away and working so hard.

CARL. What are you talking about? You'll see me every day.

63

BIRDIE. How?

CARL. You'll come out there, won't you, Birdie.

BIRDIE. Once in a while, I suppose.

CARL. I mean for good and all. We'll get married, won't we?

BIRDIE. No, no.

CARL. Sure we will. In April when the weather's getting nice. It's pretty out there in the summer, Birdie, you wouldn't believe how pretty Uncle's place is, the corn'll be coming up and there's a bit of woodland—I won't ever cut it down, Birdie, it's on a little hill, and there's a brook——

BIRDIE. Mrs. Beck wants me to go to Europe with her this summer.

CARL. Europe? Oh, hell.

BIRDIE. Italy. Fancy!

CARL. What for.

BIRDIE. Pictures and places and—oh, just Europe. You know how I like pictures, Carl.

CARL. So do I. . . . Say, Bird, I never got clear on how much you fell for England last summer.

BIRDIE. I liked it a heap.

CARL. I know, but how much. You see if we get married this spring I can't afford to take you on a wedding trip to Europe, and I'm not sure that even if I could afford it I'd want to take you.

BIRDIE. Why not, Carl?

CARL. It's got me all balled up, this Europe

business.   What's Europe got to do with us anyway?

BIRDIE. Plenty.

CARL. Plenty all right.   Why in one single day in this small town there's a famous English novelist giving out guff about the future of the English novel, there's an Englishwoman singing old English songs other side of that wall, there's an Irish guy doing the same thing down at the Catholic Club——

BIRDIE. Who?   I hadn't heard.

CARL. Dunno.   MacDermott was talking about him last night when we were playing pool. Oh, Europe is plenty with us but I'm trying to figure out why.

BIRDIE. Because we want it to be with us.

CARL. I don't.

BIRDIE. You're just ignorant, Carl Svenson, and you don't mind going on being ignorant. I'm ignorant but I *do* mind and I'm no end grateful to Mrs. Beck for giving us the chance to cultivate ourselves, having wonderful interesting people to talk at the Circle every other Thursday all through the winter.   Goodness, imagine Crampton if we hadn't the Circle and Mrs. Swaffer's Art Union and Mrs. Jackson's Study Group and Mrs. Pontofax's Little Theatre!

CARL. Crampton would be a whole lot better off without 'em.

BIRDIE. You're crude, Carl Svenson, real crude.

CARL. Maybe I am.

BIRDIE. And you don't mind being crude.

CARL. I don't know, I haven't quite figured it out yet. I know that a minute ago when I heard that music through the wall it sounded swell and whoever's singing has a darned good voice but the minute Mrs. Beck said "Old English" I just said "Hell!" quicker nor anything, and I meant it. That's the sort I am.

BIRDIE. You've a complex about Europe.

CARL. Oh, hands off the big words. Complex nothing.

BIRDIE. Yes you have a complex and I believe it's because you're raw from Europe yourself— only two generations back. Why my folks are here a hundred years and more.

CARL. Still when you went to England you felt you were going home.

BIRDIE. No I didn't. I wouldn't take a million dollars to live there, but it's lovely all the same and all Europe's lovely and you make me mad when you start sneering at culture and art and foreign travel. Hogs and corn, that's all you think of.

CARL. I think a lot about them sure enough, I have to.

BIRDIE. Of course you've your living to make, but there's other things in the world besides dollars.

CARL. Do I seem like that to you, Bird, just after dollars?

BIRDIE. Times you do. Gosh, imagine me on a farm feeding hogs and calves and talking about the weather and the crops and wondering whether the brown hen isn't laying out.

CARL. Now it's you who are being crude. You've been reading Old Homestead dope. Do you think I'd let you near my hogs? No sir, they're too valuable.

(*A bell rings.*)

BIRDIE. There he is! Where's my bag? (*She starts to hunt for it.*) Look for it, Carl, I had it a minute ago.

CARL. What do you want it for?

BIRDIE. I know I look a sight.

CARL. Show. (*He catches her, swings her face to face.*) Sure enough, you've a crumb on your cheek.

BIRDIE. Which one?

CARL. This. (*He kisses her cheek.*) Mm . . . Norah does make the nicest sandwiches.

BIRDIE. You're awful, Carl Svenson. I'm sure you've mussed me worse than ever.

CARL. Not at all. I always use kiss-proof.

(*A sound of arguing voices is heard.*)

BIRDIE. Ssh! what was that? Sounded like an argument or something. (*She cocks an ear towards the door.*)

CARL (*also listening*). That's Gordon's voice. I bet he forgot to take off Norah's overalls and Julia Beck's balling him out.

BIRDIE. Everyone's talking together.

They're coming. Now, Carl, you will behave
yourself, won't you?

CARL. Sure. I bow three times, remain
standing till the great novelist asks me to be
seated——

BIRDIE. I get so ashamed of you.

CARL. Why? Why should you mind?

BIRDIE. Oh because—because——

CARL. Because you hate to see your future
husband making a fool of himself.

BIRDIE. You have a nerve.

CARL. Well, Mrs. Svenson, I'll be as good
as gold, I'll——

BIRDIE. Ssh!   (MRS. BECK comes in.)

MRS. BECK. Birdie Cummins, what am I to
do? There's a strange Irishman at the door
trying to get in to see Miss Waters.

BIRDIE. Who is he?

MRS. BECK. That's just what I don't know.
I opened the door myself because Gordon got
all mussed up in his overalls and couldn't get
them off and there was a strange young man on
the step who said right out that he must see
Miss Waters. I said she was busy and who
was he anyway? And he said "Love" just like
that, kind of softly. And I said "What?" and
he said "Love" again and shoved his way in
and by that time Gordon had come along and
thought he was being fresh and got sort of mad
and tried to push him out but he pushed back
and Gordon fell into the grandfather clock in the

hall and cut his cheek.   And now it seems his
name *is* Love and he wasn't being fresh or anything.   He's Irish.   Who can he be, Birdie?

BIRDIE. I don't know, Mrs. Beck, I never
heard of him.

CARL. Did he say anything about the
Catholic Club?

MRS. BECK. Seems to me he did.   Said he
was singing or something.

CARL. Gordon sure has the right instinct.
I'll go help push him out.

MRS. BECK. Why?

CARL. He's another of these lecture guys.

MRS. BECK (*eagerly*). A lecturer?

CARL. Yeah.   And singing Irish folk-songs.

MRS. BECK. Why, how perfectly lovely.   I'll
bring him right in.

CARL. Mrs. Beck—for the love of Mike—
aren't two enough?

MRS. BECK (*hurrying out*). Why, my grandmother was Irish.

CARL. Lordy God, this is going to be some
evening.   Julia Beck has surely got Mabel
Swaffer backed off the map for tonight anyway.

BIRDIE. Yeah, after this one Mabel'll have to
give her best. (*She is vaguely looking for her
bag.*)   I adore the Irish.

CARL. Oh, of course.   Anything that isn't
Yankee.

BIRDIE. Swedes aren't so bad.

CARL. Even Americanised ones?

BIRDIE. They're nicest of all.

CARL. There's one who wants to go dancing with you right now.

BIRDIE. I couldn't, Carl. I wouldn't miss this evening, not for anything. But you go if you like.

CARL. No, I'll stay, I'll try and get a little culture.

BIRDIE. You're so conceited, playing at being low-brow and knowing perfectly well that you've got more brains than all of us put together. You're too simple, we've all got your number.

> (MRS. BECK *comes back followed by* MICHAEL LOVE *and* GORDON. MICHAEL *is not in evening dress, he wears a dark suit and a soft white shirt.* GORDON *holds a handkerchief to his cheek.*)

MRS. BECK. Let me present Miss Cummins, Mr. Love.

MICHAEL. How do you do?

BIRDIE. Pleased to meet you, Mr. Love.

MRS. BECK. And Mr. Svenson.

MICHAEL. How do you do?

CARL (*with no manners*). Howdy?

MRS. BECK. I don't think Mr. Love will ever forget the way he was received here, he'll surely have something against Crampton for the rest of his natural life. But Mr. Beck gets just so passionate——

> (*Little* GORDON *smirks, puffs himself out.*)

MICHAEL. I'm afraid it was my fault entirely

70

crashing in like this, but I felt I couldn't miss the chance of seeing Miss Waters.

GORDON. And you remember in Rome, dearest, four years ago?

MRS. BECK. I shall never forget it, Mr. Love. In the Borghese Gardens, six o'clock in the evening, broad daylight. Well, Mr. Beck just told the man he'd go straight to the Consul. Those Romans, they're so passionate, they just can't hold themselves in. But of course the Irish are different and it was very very silly of Mr. Beck to——

GORDON (*cocking an ear to the door*). Darling, the clock.

MRS. BECK. What clock?

GORDON. The grandfather. Striking!

MRS. BECK. Gracious goodness, and it's beside the door, it'll just kill Miss Waters' talk. Put rugs over it, Gordon, sit on it—hurry.

GORDON. Yes, dearest. (*He hurries out.*)

MRS. BECK (*calling after him*). And put a bit of court plaster on your face, it's in the kitchen, you can fix it while you're sitting on the clock.

GORDON'S VOICE. Yes, dearest.

MRS. BECK. That clock is the quaintest old clock you ever saw, it doesn't go but if it gets a jolt or anything it starts striking and it goes on and goes on and goes on.

MICHAEL. My fault again, Mrs. Beck, I pushed your husband against it. Maybe I should help sit on it.

MRS. BECK. No, no, Gordon'll manage—but perhaps I'd better get a pillow—if you'll excuse me just a minute. (*She hurries out.*)

BIRDIE. Won't you sit down, Mr. Love, and have a sandwich?

MICHAEL (*sitting and eating*). Thanks.

BIRDIE. You're a friend of Miss Waters?

MICHAEL. We travelled out on the same ship.

BIRDIE. Oh, so did Mr. Chesterfield Wragsdale, I suppose you know him too. He's coming tonight.

MICHAEL. Here?

BIRDIE. You don't mind, do you?

MICHAEL. Not at all.

BIRDIE. Ah, you English and Irish! I only heard about your lecture a few minutes ago. I wish I could have heard it. I had an Irish grandmother.

MICHAEL. Is that so? But why aren't you listening to Miss Waters?

BIRDIE. I couldn't. I came too late.

MICHAEL (*to* CARL). And you?

CARL (*acting the boob*). I wouldn't understand it. I'm stoopid.

MICHAEL (*speaking rather artificially*). Mine isn't at all a serious lecture, it's just a little talk about Ireland, an attempt to make you visualise the island of saints and scholars, the dream-island, the island of the poets; I illustrate my lecture by poems and songs.

BIRDIE. Ah, your Irish poets! Aren't they too wonderful?

MICHAEL (*dreamily*). The old country ballads, and then Yeats, A. E., Padraic Colum—" I will arise and go now, and go to Innisfree."

BIRDIE. Oh, doesn't it make you want to go? If only my girls could hear you.

MICHAEL (*dropping his dream-voice and becoming quite practical*). Your girls?

BIRDIE. I teach school here. I have the English class.

MICHAEL. I wish I could talk to them.

BIRDIE. I wish you could.

MICHAEL. I'd like to tell them about Ireland.

BIRDIE. They ought to know. We're so ignorant here, Mr. Love——

MICHAEL. What about tomorrow morning? I'm not leaving Crampton till eleven-forty-five.

BIRDIE (*a little overwhelmed at the way she is being rushed*). Oh, but how perfectly lovely!

MICHAEL. Can you arrange it?

BIRDIE. We do try to get lecturers from time to time but we've so little money——

MICHAEL. I like speaking to schools, catching the young American mind while it's pliable; you can pay me almost nothing at all.

BIRDIE. I'd be ashamed to say how little we can afford.

MICHAEL. A hundred dollars?

BIRDIE (*shaking her head*). I'm afraid not.

MICHAEL. Fifty? I'd come for fifty.

BIRDIE. We could manage that. Oh, it seems such a mean little sum——

MICHAEL. Don't mention it. What hour?

BIRDIE. It must be between nine-thirty and ten-fifteen.

MICHAEL. Can you call for me?

BIRDIE. Yeah, of course.

MICHAEL (*his diary out*). My address is 2264 Ninth Street, I'm staying with people called Burke, their telephone number is Central 6144 —I'm writing it down for you so that you won't forget.

BIRDIE. Oh, I won't forget. Ninth Street is quite near the school, I'll call for you a few minutes after nine, you'd like to look round the school before your talk and meet the teachers, wouldn't you?

MICHAEL. Of course. (*Handing her a card on which he has been writing.*) There.

MRS. BECK'S VOICE. Birdie Cummins!

BIRDIE. Yeah, Mrs. Beck.

MRS. BECK'S VOICE. Come here a minute.

BIRDIE. Coming. (*She goes out.*)

CARL. Well I got to hand it to you.

MICHAEL. What do you mean?

CARL. The way you landed that lecture! You ought to be selling cars or victrolas or something. You're surely thrown away lecturing.

MICHAEL. That's what I'm thinking. Know of a decent opening?

CARL. No.

MICHAEL. But this is a live young town.

CARL. I'm a farmer.

MICHAEL. Oh Lord! I used to be.

CARL. Why did you quit?

MICHAEL. Too damned slow.

CARL. Do you get a kick out of lecturing?

MICHAEL. Not what you'd call a kick. I do it to earn a few dollars. Do you get a kick out of farming?

CARL. Yeah.

MICHAEL. That's fine. It's a great country all around here.

CARL. You can cut that stuff right out, you won't get a date from me.

MICHAEL. I wasn't trying to. As a matter of fact I mean what I say—for once.

CARL. And you'd be surprised to hear that I know Yeats' stuff as well as you—maybe better.

MICHAEL. That's easy. I mugged him up on the boat coming across.

CARL. I bet that's a lie.

MICHAEL. Had you an Irish grandmother?

CARL. No.

MICHAEL. Thank God. Who was that old Irishwoman, anyway, who went all over the States fifty years ago dropping children to right and left?

CARL (*laughing*). I like you, I don't know why.

MICHAEL. So do I. Can't we have a talk?

75

CARL. Not a chance here with all these dames. Like a drink?

MICHAEL. Don't torture me.

CARL. I'll stick on here till you're through. Then I'll take you to a place I know. Say, what do you think of that fellow Shaw?

MICHAEL. Bernard? Oh, I think he's——

BIRDIE (*hurrying in*). I silenced that clock, I hit it in the middle of its face and it went dumb. And Mr. Wragsdale has arrived and you could look at my nose and shave by it. (*She looks vaguely for her bag.*)

MICHAEL. Is this what you're wanting? (*He takes her bag from the dresser.*)

BIRDIE. Well, what do you think of that, Carl Svenson? God bless you Mr. Love, as they say in Ireland. (*She starts on her face.*)

MICHAEL (*to* CARL). Remember, Wragsdale doesn't lecture for dollars, he does it because he has something big and beautiful to give you.

CARL. I suspected that.

MICHAEL. But he's not a bad chap.

> (MRS. BECK *bustles in followed by* WRAGS-
> DALE *and* GORDON—*by now sticking-
> plastered.* WRAGSDALE *is beautiful in a
> dinner jacket.*)

MRS. BECK. Meet my friend Miss Cummins, Mr. Wragsdale, she was teaching school this afternoon and unfortunately missed your lecture.

WRAGSDALE. How do you do, Miss Cummins?

BIRDIE (*shaking hands*). I'm so glad to meet

you, Mr. Wragsdale. Your acquaintance is a pleasure I'm sure. If I didn't hear you talk I've surely read you, every word of you.

MRS. BECK. And this is Mr. Carl Svenson, literature's not much in his line I'm afraid.

WRAGSDALE. How do you do? (*They shake hands.* CARL *says nothing.*)

MICHAEL (*coming forward*). Hullo !

WRAGSDALE. Why, Love ! Who'd think of seeing *you* here ? You've been lecturing I suppose ?

MICHAEL. Yes, to the Catholic Club here.

MRS. BECK. They have the most interesting people, Mr. Wragsdale, I often go myself—don't I, Gordon ? They made me an honorary member though I'm not a Catholic in recognition of the big work the Circle's doing—wasn't that sweet of them ? Of course I couldn't go tonight with Miss Waters here but I'm hoping that before the evening is over we'll have a few words from Mr. Love about Ireland and the message it has to give the world.

MICHAEL. Oh, Mrs. Beck, I only came in to see Miss Waters.

MRS. BECK (*archly*). You knocked my husband down to see Miss Waters ! I know ! Well, when England and Ireland fall in love with each other there's the end of the Irish question—that's what I always say. But what do you think of my little corner of Old England, Mr. Wragsdale ?

WRAGSDALE. Little . . . Old England ?

MRS. BECK. Isn't this the quaintest little narrow room you ever saw ? I gave Mr. Beck no rest day or night till he'd make it for me. It's sliced off the top of our big room. The other side of that wall is as American as you please but right here, in this corner, I'm in England. I come in here and Crampton's left behind, the whole width of the Atlantic stretches between me and the other side of that wall. That old fireplace—look at it—I got that in Gloucestershire, yanked it straight out of a farmhouse ; that old dresser I got in New York, it was only landed two days. I had it fixed up for books and china. Isn't it the nicest thing you ever saw ? And the china's all old English —aren't those Chelsea figures sweet, and the Wedgwood ? And those fire-dogs, and the pewter ? Mabel Swaffer goes in for old English silver but I'd rather have my pewter, it—it's so homey, it sort of speaks to me.

WRAGSDALE. Charming, charming.

MRS. BECK. Don't you feel now you're right at home ? If you were staying for one day I'm sure you'd be stealing in here, setting in that old chair and writing a novel. You just couldn't resist it.

WRAGSDALE. Delightful! And how wonderful to find it here, in your great middle-west.

MRS. BECK. And look at the books, Mr. Wragsdale. All English. I wouldn't let a foreign book in here for fear the atmosphere might go. I've got all the dear old English books, Sterne right down to Hardy and yourself —no, I think you're borrowed at the moment— there's such a run on you, Mr. Wragsdale. Don't you think Hardy's the most English thing ever was?

WRAGSDALE. A wonderful artist. Such atmosphere——

MRS. BECK. Atmosphere! That's just the word. Those moors—can't you feel them under your feet? I say to Mr. Beck " Well, you can't get away from it, Thomas Hardy's English, one hundred per cent. English." And Jane Austen, ain't she—*isn't* she quaint? I know some people don't fall for Jane—Mr. Beck don't for one—but I always say to him " Well, Mr. Beck, she's unique, you can't get away from that, she's unique."

BIRDIE. I think Jane's a mite slow.

WRAGSDALE. Ah, you young Americans!

CARL. Birdie, not a word against Janey.

MRS. BECK. And look at the pictures. Look at those huntsmen. Doesn't that bring you straight back to Jorrocks and Mr. Sponge? And aren't the Lovat Frasers cute? Mr. Beck gave me that one for my birthday.

GORDON. No, darling, it was the other.

MRS. BECK. Was it, dearest? And I gave him the funniest little Madonna I picked up in New York. Mr. Beck is crazy about Italy,

Mr. Wragsdale, that's why we're going there this summer. You'll have to get him to show you his study, it's just a little corner of Italy.

WRAGSDALE. How wonderful! Italy and England in Crampton!

MRS. BECK. Yes, indeed. This room is inspirational, Mr. Wragsdale. Why it was here, setting on that chair back of Birdie Cummins that I got the idea of the Circle.

WRAGSDALE. The Circle?

MRS. BECK. This group of women who meet here every other Thursday—Miss Waters is giving them a talk just the other side of that door. (*She points to the panelled wall.*) I don't suppose you'd guess that that was a door, but it is—that is the wall slides right back. At first I had only a curtained opening but I felt something was wrong, I didn't quite know what, then I chanced on a book of Henry James and he put me right. He said the most un-European thing about our houses was that we had no doors to our rooms so I walked straight out and had that sliding wall fixed.

CARL (*drily*). It keeps in the atmosphere.

MRS. BECK. It surely does, Carl. Don't you think atmosphere's the most important thing, Mr. Wragsdale? But of course you do. There was so much atmosphere in that lovely talk you gave us this afternoon.

WRAGSDALE. Was there? I'm so glad.

MRS. BECK. There certainly was. Maybe you don't know it yourself but you couldn't get up on a platform without being—being——

CARL. Atmospheric.

MRS. BECK. Yeah, Carl, atmospheric. There's Mr. Love—why, just to look at him you can feel the bogs and the mountains and the old songs and the shamrocks.

MICHAEL (*affecting modesty*). Oh, Mrs. Beck !

MRS. BECK. Oh, I should say so. The very minute you met him, Gordon, didn't you feel how 'Irish he was ?

GORDON. I certainly did.

MRS. BECK. That cut on his cheek, Mr. Wragsdale—Mr. Love gave him that, he pushed him into the clock. Isn't that the quaintest, most Irish thing ? . . . Ssh ! . . . There's Miss Waters singing again. (*They listen in silence for half a minute.*)

MICHAEL (*involuntarily*). Merciful God !

MRS. BECK. What ?

MICHAEL. The nerve of her ! The—the cheek of her !

MRS. BECK. What do you mean ?

MICHAEL. It's an Irish song. I sang it to her on the boat. Don't you remember, Wragsdale?

WRAGSDALE. No.

> (*It is indeed " The Maid of the Sweet Brown Knowe " sung well but with an unmistakable English lilt to it in spite of a strong brogue.*)

MRS. BECK. Isn't it charming? The Little Wild English Rose! You must come and hear her, Mr. Love.

MICHAEL. No, no, please.

CARL. Can't you think how it will help the atmosphere to have a real Irishman in the audience?

MRS. BECK. Yes indeed, Carl. We'll slip in the back, Mr. Love, we'll not disturb anyone. Come along. Excuse me just a minute, Mr. Wragsdale, I'll park Mr. Love in the Circle and then I'll be right back. Gordon, the fruit cocktails. (*She drags* MICHAEL *out.*)

GORDON. Right away, darling. (*He goes out too.*)

BIRDIE. Won't you sit down, Mr. Wragsdale.

WRAGSDALE. May I just, for a moment, stand and stare. It *is* wonderful. (*He looks again at the fireplace, the books, the pictures.*) And touching, touching.

BIRDIE. Julia Beck is a wonderful woman, one of the most wonderful women in Crampton.

WRAGSDALE. Please tell me about Crampton, I don't think I've ever before lectured in such a comparatively small town. My agent generally makes me stick to big cities and the universities.

BIRDIE. What's there to tell about Crampton, Carl? Nothing, I guess.

CARL. Twenty-five years ago it was a cluster of shacks round a saloon and a railroad depot, last census gave us two hundred thousand, next census will see us almost doubled. There's that to tell for one thing.

WRAGSDALE. And why, why this quick increase?

CARL. Well, we make the Peak Car.

WRAGSDALE. The Peak? I don't think I know it.

BIRDIE. Not know the Peak?

CARL. It's the dandiest car on the market—at the price.

WRAGSDALE. You're in the motor business I suppose.

CARL. No sir, I'm a farmer.

WRAGSDALE. What an extraordinarily ugly country it is all round here.

CARL. Of course it's bare in winter. You should see it in spring and summer—it's fine then.

WRAGSDALE. Yes. But even in winter the English country is charming.

CARL. This isn't England.

WRAGSDALE. I realise that. In spite of Mrs. Beck's efforts!

CARL. Oh, Julia Beck! That woman makes me sick.

BIRDIE. Ssh, Carl, she might hear. Or Gordon.

CARL. What of it.

WRAGSDALE. It *is* a little absurd—all this. (*He indicates the " English Corner."*)

CARL. Absurd? It's plumb crazy.

WRAGSDALE. But it all fits in with your craving for Europe.

CARL. I'm not craving for Europe.

BIRDIE (*a little anxiously*). Carl's a great American, but he's not as narrow as he makes out to be.

WRAGSDALE. I can see the ultra-American point of view but I can't much sympathise with it; I believe you will only find content, ultimate content when you have managed to realise that you are really Europeans.

CARL. You mean English?

WRAGSDALE. Well, let's say Anglo-Saxons. After all, you speak our language.

CARL. Less and less. I don't believe that in fifteen years you've added more than fifteen words to the English language, I bet we add about a hundred words a year. In fifty years we'll have a new language.

WRAGSDALE. You think you're growing away from Europe, not towards it?

CARL. I hope so.

BIRDIE. You're narrow, Carl Svenson, just narrow.

CARL. How do you mean, narrow?

BIRDIE. Maybe you're not narrow. I know what you are, you're scared.

CARL. Scared? Me? What of?

BIRDIE. Europe.

CARL (*after a pause*). Maybe I am.

WRAGSDALE. Now that's very interesting. Why?

CARL. I don't know that I can tell you but it's something like this : you can come out here lecturing for three months or half a year and you'll go back same as you came out ; we go to Europe and it knocks us dizzy. We go to Paris to learn to paint and we go rotten over drink and women, we go to Italy for a month and we babble for years about the sunsets from the Lido, the Titian blue and all the rest of it, we go to Spain and get all goofy about El Greco and forget the Spanish-American war, we go to England and the result is Julia Beck's "English corner." There are some people who can't get drunk like gentlemen, we can't take Europe like gentlemen so we'd better lay off it till we can. Scared? I guess I am scared of Europe standing here in this corner of Old England.

WRAGSDALE. It's not Europe that's responsible for this room, it's Crampton.

CARL. What's poor old Crampton got to do with it?

WRAGSDALE. It's just because it's not poor "old" Crampton. It's not old. Twenty-five or thirty years at the most, with no background, no tradition, no memory.

CARL. You'll be talking of "atmosphere" in a minute.

WRAGSDALE. I will, and not a bit ashamed of the word. There is no atmosphere here.

CARL. What's your background?

WRAGSDALE. Generations of English men and women stretching back for hundreds of years. Never very distinguished, the army— but rarely a general, the church—nothing higher than a dean, the law—only a few judges, but always a tradition of culture, of decent living, old houses, old furniture, old books, an un- broken heritage handed down from generation to generation gathering gradually a patina, a tradition.

CARL. I can beat you for tradition. I'm a farmer, so's my dad, so's my grand-dad and back as far as you care to count. Your people have been lawyers and clergymen and what-not, mine have been farmers right back to the Garden of Eden I guess. He came out here, my grand-dad did and his three brothers, straight from a farm in Sweden, straight to the land here. They cleared it, built a shack, got a few hogs, a patch of corn, then more hogs, more corn, then they knocked down the shacks and built themselves houses. Tradition! Those farms are pure Svenson. Svenson muscle and Svenson sweat has gone to the making of every blamed acre of them. We've married there, bred there, died there, and you've the nerve to tell me we've neither atmosphere nor tradition.

WRAGSDALE. It's different.

CARL. Sure it's different, it's American.

WRAGSDALE. Yet Mrs. Beck and millions of

other Mrs. Becks stretch out eager hands to Europe.

CARL. They're old and they're idle. I'm young and busy. Europe's just a light woman, and that kind's dangerous.

WRAGSDALE. You're rather exceptional you know.

CARL. Not at all, there's millions of young Americans like me but you don't meet us, my sort don't go to your lectures, we don't need to.

WRAGSDALE. You know everything? Lucky young men!

CARL. We know that one of these days we'll be standing over you counting you out?

WRAGSDALE. Counting Europe out?

CARL. Counting England out, we can give the rest of Europe the go-by.

WRAGSDALE. Are you one of those strange Americans who want to fight England?

CARL. Sure I do.

WRAGSDALE. Now I wonder why.

CARL. We've got to lick you for our own sakes ; we'll be grown up when you holler you've had enough.

WRAGSDALE. Isn't it enough that you beat us once before?

CARL. No, that was only a little family affair —purely English. The next time it will be the British Empire against the American Nation and when you sign our terms of peace we *will* be a Nation and maybe then we can think about being friends.

WRAGSDALE (*really troubled*). I can't bear to hear you saying that. One of the reasons that brings me to the States is to do my bit to better the relations between the two countries.

CARL. Forget it, you can't. Maybe your coming makes them worse.

BIRDIE. Carl!

CARL. I don't mean to be rude, I'm not meaning anything personal, but the more some of us see of you——

WRAGSDALE. Ten years ago we bled and died in the same cause.

CARL. And most of us will never forgive you for that.

WRAGSDALE. Forgive? Is forgiveness necessary?

CARL. Surely. We were tricked into it, we won the damned thing for you.

WRAGSDALE. Please!

CARL. Oh, I know. According to you we came in at the last lap, but would it have been the last lap if we hadn't come in? And what have you to show for it all? More'n a million dead and you owe us about three billion dollars.

WRAGSDALE. Can't you imagine that it might be necessary for us to, in your phrase, count Germany out?

CARL. It don't look as if you had succeeded.

What did we have on Germany anyway? Our war won't be like that, it will be a sort of holy war.

WRAGSDALE. Holy war! Those words seem to me to be so antagonistic that they should never be used together.

CARL. Why not? When it's a war to make a country's soul? You won't admit that we've got a soul of our own, we're only some kind of ignorant country cousins to you, we've got to show you that we're as different from you as an oak tree is from an automobile.

WRAGSDALE. Can't we learn to admit the difference without having a war?

CARL. No, you only respect the fellow who knocks you down. Look at Ireland, she was a sort of comic strip in a newspaper, until she bested you.

MRS. BECK (*coming in*). That's her last song, she told me she'd do a verse of " Auld Lang Syne " to finish up with, and Gordon's got everything fixed. I wish you could see her, Mr. Wragsdale, she looks so Scotch I got quite carried away. I think she's one of the most perfect artistes we've ever had here. (*" Auld Lang Syne " has begun and has been faintly heard during the end of the conversation between* CARL *and* WRAGSDALE. *Now it terminates and a burst of faint applause is heard.*)

MRS. BECK. Listen to that! Crampton's tribute to England's art! Isn't it wonderful?

BIRDIE. I'll go give Gordon a hand. Come on Carl and make yourself useful.

(*She and* CARL *go out.*)

WRAGSDALE. He's a curious type.

MRS. BECK. He's just crude, Mr. Wragsdale, you mustn't mind him. . . . Now Mr. Love is going to bring Miss Waters straight here as soon as those women will let her by. I should think they'd want to eat her after the lovely talk she's given them. (*Calling.*) Gordon!

GORDON (*putting in his head*). Dearest?

MRS. BECK. Send us in some coffee, darling.

GORDON. Certainly. (*He disappears.*)

MRS. BECK. I thought you'd rather stay quietly here in the background, I'm sure all those women this afternoon wore you out. I always say that in the old days people were thrown to the lions but nowadays we throw the lions to the people. I haven't told the Circle yet that you're here, it'll be the nicest surprise for them. They'll be just crazy to hear you.

WRAGSDALE. Oh, but I said I wouldn't speak, you promised that I shouldn't be asked to.

MRS. BECK. You mustn't speak, I wouldn't let you, but you'll just share your message with us, won't you?

WRAGSDALE. Oh, really, Mrs. Beck——

MRS. BECK. I won't tease you now but I think when you meet these women and see how simple and sincere we all are you'll feel you must give us a few words, something inspirational you know, something we can take away with us and think about—ah, here is the heroine of the evening.

> (VIVIENNE *and* MICHAEL *come in. She looks charming in her eighteenth-century dress. She has a small plaid shawl on her arm.*)

VIVIENNE (*gushing*). Dear Mrs. Beck! Such a wonderful evening, such a wonderful audience! Ah, Mr. Wragsdale, isn't it nice to meet you again? Mr. Love told me that you were here. I was afraid there wasn't a chance of our meeting in this great big wonderful country.

MRS. BECK. How did you like your audience?

VIVIENNE. It was perfectly wonderful. I felt so shy at first—I always do——

MRS. BECK. Ah, you little Wild English Rose!

VIVIENNE. But they were so sympathetic, it was like talking to friends. Don't you find American audiences wonderful, Mr. Wragsdale?

WRAGSDALE. Yes. You're enjoying it all then?

VIVIENNE. I adore it. But I've adored no where as much as Crampton, Mrs. Beck has been so sweet to me. (*She presses, almost embraces her.*)

MRS. BECK. We loved her the moment we saw her, Mr. Wragsdale, you should hear the things Mr. Beck says about her. It's a good thing I'm not a jealous woman. We'd like to keep her with us always.

VIVIENNE. Oh, Mrs. Beck! You make me feel shy.

MRS. BECK. You're the freshest daintiest thing. And so English!

MICHAEL (*a little grimly*). Singing Irish songs!

VIVIENNE. That's cruel of you. Wasn't it dreadful, Mr. Wragsdale, to get caught out like that? Was it very awful, Mr. Love?

MICHAEL. Not at all. It sounded grand.

VIVIENNE. You know people love my Irish songs, Mr. Love, they really do. I put this shawl over my head—so—now don't I look like a regular colleen from the auld countrie?

WRAGSDALE. Charming!

VIVIENNE (*in her heaviest brogue*). Arrah, git along wid you! It's joking me you are.

MRS. BECK. Isn't she cute?

GORDON (*his head through the door, confidentially*). Darling!

MRS. BECK. Yes, Gordon, we're ready for the coffee.

GORDON. Darling!

MRS. BECK. As quick as you can for those Negroes will be here any minute.

GORDON. No spoons.

MRS. BECK. They're in the kitchen, on the table.

GORDON. I've looked, they're not.

MRS. BECK. Oh—excuse me just a minute, Mr. Wragsdale, my coloured girl walked out this evening and poor Gordon is so stupid about things——

GORDON (*reproachfully*). Dearest!

MRS. BECK. Never mind, darling, come along and I'll show you where the silly spoons are. (*They go out.*)

WRAGSDALE. ⎫
MICHAEL.   ⎬ Well?
VIVIENNE. ⎭

(*Unconsciously but quite noticeably all relax,* VIVIENNE *ceases to gush,* WRAGSDALE *is less portentous,* MICHAEL *less romantic.*)

VIVIENNE. It *is* nice to see you both. Oh, if we could only get away together and have a whole evening of it.

WRAGSDALE. So you're not enjoying it?

VIVIENNE. I am, I am. But I feel sometimes as if my mouth would break.

MICHAEL. Talking?

VIVIENNE. Smiling. I'm being the charming ingenuous English girl from morning to night.

WRAGSDALE. Well, that's what you are.

VIVIENNE. Oh, Mr. Wragsdale, I'm not as ingenuous as I look. I hope I don't consciously play-act but people expect a certain kind of thing from me and I find myself giving it to them. I lie awake at night and blush at all the wild-English-rose things I've said and done during the day. (*To* WRAGSDALE.) Don't *you* lie in bed and blush?

WRAGSDALE. Certainly not.

MICHAEL. I play-act but I don't blush. From dewy dawn to rosy eve I'm the dreamy young Irishman. They want it like that and I'll give them as much as they'll take so long as they pay me for it.

WRAGSDALE. Are you making much?

MICHAEL. Yes. Oh, maybe you wouldn't call it much. I'll go anywhere for my expenses and fifty dollars.

WRAGSDALE (*shocked*). Fifty dollars.!

MICHAEL. I suppose I'm shockingly cheapening the market but I've no agent so everything goes straight into my pocket. Since I blew in here this evening I booked a fifty dollar talk tomorrow morning. I've made all I came out to make and now I've a month more to stay and make something for myself.

VIVIENNE. My agent says I've done very well considering that people knew nothing about me. I'm to come out next autumn for a tour right across to the coast.

WRAGSDALE. I'm delighted to hear that.

VIVIENNE. You've done splendidly, I suppose?

WRAGSDALE. Oh, just as usual. I confess I'll be glad when it's over.

MICHAEL. You sail back with me in a month's time on the *Terrific*.

WRAGSDALE. Yes, I'm sailing on the *Terrific*. But how did you know?

MICHAEL. Nicholas Brice wrote and told me. (*To* VIVIENNE.) When do you sail?

VIVIENNE. In three weeks. On the *Tremendaria*.

MICHAEL. Cancel your passage and come with us.

VIVIENNE. Wouldn't that be fun? I might, if I could fill in the week with a recital or two that would pay my hotel bill.

MICHAEL. I've a sort of cousin in New York who might fix up something for you with an Irish club there.

VIVIENNE. Ah, they wouldn't like my old English songs and I'd never dare to sing them my Irish ones.

MICHAEL. Oh, they'll love your colleen stuff. *I* know. Do stay. Nicholas Brice is throwing a party for Mr. Wragsdale and me the night before we sail.

WRAGSDALE. Is he?

MICHAEL. Yes. I had a letter from him this morning, I had told him when I was sailing and he said you were going on the same ship——

WRAGSDALE. Yes, I offered myself to him for a night or two before I sailed.

MICHAEL. So he says he'll give us supper just before we go on board and Molly'll be there and I know he'll love to have Miss Waters—— !

VIVIENNE. Molly? That was the little Irish girl wasn't it?

MICHAEL. Yes, Molly O'Sullivan. I suppose you pinched her song too?

VIVIENNE. I'm afraid I did.

MICHAEL. You're shameless.

VIVIENNE. Not at all! But I thought Miss O'Sullivan would have gone home long ago. Wasn't she only coming to New York to bring some children back to Ireland?

MICHAEL. She gave up that idea. She's settled in New York.

VIVIENNE. Oh. Got married?

MICHAEL. No, just stopped on. I've only seen her once or twice but we write to each other. (*With exaggerated American accent.*) Say, won't it be bully to get back?

VIVIENNE (*with the same accent*). It sure will. (*Recollecting herself.*) Oh, I must be careful. You know after I'd been a week in America I fell in love with the accent and all the queer slang and kept on using it and my agent had to talk to me quite seriously and say that my tour was ruined if I was anything but a little Wild English Rose. But sometimes I forget. Don't you find yourself dropping into Americanese, Mr. Wragsdale?

WRAGSDALE. I don't think so. No, I'm sure I don't.

VIVIENNE. I suppose *you* wouldn't. Tell me, what do you want first and most when you get to England? I know what I want. A cup——

WRAGSDALE. ——of——

MICHAEL. ——tea.

VIVIENNE. Not "English breakfast" or Souchong or Wowwow, just plain tee ee ay. And I'm not going to shake anyone's hand for months and months, and if anyone says "pleased to meet you" I'll smack them in the face. And isn't it horrid of me to say that, here, in this house? For there's more personal kindness in any square mile of America than in any twenty miles of England—and when I say that I'm not being a Wild English Rose.

WRAGSDALE. Certainly, they're kind.

VIVIENNE. Perhaps it's the drop of Irish that is in most of them, is it, Mr. Love? Isn't Ireland all loving-kindness and gun-men?

MICHAEL. I haven't met with much Irish loving-kindness in Ireland; America has us beaten to the ropes. And for the love of God don't talk to me about their drop of Irish. You'll be mentioning in a minute that Irish grandmother.

(MRS. BECK *comes in followed by* GORDON *with a tray of coffee.*)

MRS. BECK. I don't know what you'll think of me for leaving you like this, but I'm sure you've had a lovely talk and now you'll be longing for a cup of coffee. Hand the coffee round, Gordon. (*He does so.*) I've been talking to a few of the Circle, Mr. Love, and they're crazy to hear you sing.

MICHAEL. Oh, Mrs. Beck, I couldn't——

MRS. BECK. Why, whatever's happened to

the sandwiches, Gordon, there are only a couple left?

BIRDIE (*coming in with* CARL, *both carry plates of cakes*). I believe Carl and I ate all the sandwiches.

MRS. BECK. Well, Birdie Cummins! And those were made specially for Mr. Wragsdale and Miss Waters.

BIRDIE. Here's a dandy iced cake. (*The food is handed round.*)

MRS. BECK. There's an old lady here, Mr. Love, a Mrs. Hoffmann, I guess she's close on eighty but she's really awfully spry, she's a lovely person, ain't she, Birdie?—well, she's longing to meet you. Her grandmother was from Kerry County.

MICHAEL. Was she really?

(*Four Negroes come in.*)

MRS. BECK. I declare! Here's Mr. Jackson. How do you do, Mr. Jackson? (*She doesn't shake hands.*) I'm so very glad you were able to come.

MR. JACKSON. We're surely pleased to be here, Mrs. Beck.

MRS. BECK. I want to present you to Mr. Chesterfield Wragsdale, the great English novelist.

MR. JACKSON. I'm pleased to meet you, Mr. Chesterfield Wragsdale.

WRAGSDALE (*shaking hands*). How do you do?

MRS. BECK. And this is Miss Vivienne Waters, the little Wild Rose of Old England, she's crazy to hear your songs.

MR. JACKSON. Pleased to meet you, Miss Vivienne Waters.

VIVIENNE (*shaking hands*). How do you do?

MRS. BECK. And this is Mr. Michael Love, he's Irish and he sings too.

MR. JACKSON. Pleased to meet you, Mr. Michael Love.

MICHAEL (*shaking hands*). How do you do?

MRS. BECK. And now will you please introduce your friends, Mr. Jackson.

> (MR. JACKSON *punctiliously introduces the three other singers*—MR. GEORGE BROWN, MR. ALEXANDER JOHNSON *and* MR. SEPTIMUS LEE. *Each Negro says "Pleased to meet you," mentioning the name of the person to whom he is being introduced; each European says "How do you do?" and shakes hands with exaggerated courtesy to show that no colour prejudice exists. The performance of these introductions is quite mechanical, every movement, every intonation is an exact reproduction of the preceding one.*)

MR. JACKSON (*when this is over*). I'm afraid we're kind of early, Mrs. Beck——

MRS. BECK. Not at all, Mr. Jackson.

MR. JACKSON. But as I told you we're due at the soirée at the Baptist Church. We're due

there right now.   We'd like to sing just as soon
as we can and get across to the Church.

MRS. BECK. I know, Mr. Jackson, we only
wish you could stay all evening.

MR. JACKSON. If we could sing now, Mrs.
Beck, and get away, there's a whole long
programme at the soirée.

MRS. BECK. Well, that's a mite awkward.
I'm afraid the Circle's not through with their
refreshments.   Would it put you out if they
went on eating while you're singing?

MR. JACKSON. No ma'am, not at all.   I'm
sorry to rush you all like this, Mrs. Beck, but
I told you how we were circumstanced.   We'd
fixed this thing with the Church before we got
your invitation——

MRS. BECK. I know.   Why, that will be all
right.   Gordon, move back the door.   Now
I want you all to get over this side of the
room.

> (*She shepherds everyone into the " English
> Corner."*   GORDON *goes to the side of the
> panelled opening and presses a button.
> Noiselessly the panelled wall slides to the
> left and now half the stage reveals a large
> inner room.   The floor of the room is
> raked, higher at the back than at the
> front and tilted to the left.   The room is
> crowded with people, all women.   These
> women are represented by puppets, four
> types repeated again and again—the old,*

the middle-aged, the woman of twenty-three and the girl of eighteen. Each puppet carries in its hands a plate and a spoon; on the plate is presumably ice-cream. The scene is quite non-realistic; the puppets are cut in the flat out of thin wood, but they are life-size. The rake of the floor and the tilt to the left make it all odd and amusing.)

MRS. BECK (*advancing to the opening and addressing the puppets*). Friends, I've got three big surprises for you tonight and like a good showman—or show-woman I ought to say—I'm going to introduce them to you one by one. You've already shared in one of the most wonderful evenings this Circle has ever had. We've all listened spellbound to Miss Vivienne Waters, the Wild Rose of Old England, and I'd say that Miss Waters and her songs have given us tonight a new slant on England.

THE PUPPETS (*artificially*). Yes, yes, yessss.

MRS. BECK. I knew, friends, you'd feel like that about it. Now we're going to show Miss Waters that we have right here in our own country a native flower, as native to our soil as the rose is to England. I am very very proud tonight to bring you and Miss Waters in touch with something which is native to America, something which comes from our own coloured Baptist Church on Tenth Street—the Baptist Quartet, led by Mr. Jackson.

(*She sweeps the Negroes into the opening. They bow.*)

THE PUPPETS (*purring with pleasure*). Ahhhh !

MRS. BECK. Mr. Jackson and his friends are in a hurry to get away so I'm going to ask them to sing now but you can go right on with your refreshments.   Now, Mr. Jackson.

(*She retires to the " English Corner." The Negroes sing a spiritual, it is beautifully sung.   At the end of each verse each puppet mechanically raises the spoon to its mouth and then returns it to its plate.*)

THE PUPPETS (*when the spiritual is ended*). Ahhhh !

MRS. BECK. Thank you, Mr. Jackson.   Now we'd like a solo or a duet.

(*A solo or duet follows.   The puppets eat ice-cream and applaud exactly as before.*)

MRS. BECK (*advancing into the opening*).   Now friends, I'm sorry to say that this quartet can't be with us for more than another few minutes so I'm going to ask them to step across into the parlour and continue their programme there. Any of you who want to get better acquainted with our genuine American Negro songs will follow them. . . .   Thank you so much, Mr. Jackson, right through there across the hall. (*The Negroes go out.*)   Now friends, that was my first surprise and maybe it wasn't much of a surprise because I think most of you knew you were going to hear the Baptist Quartet.

But my next surprise will be genuine. We've had England with us this evening and our thoughts have been way across the Atlantic, thousands of miles from Crampton. Well, generally when we go to Europe, first bit of land we see after leaving the States is a little green island. It's just the littlest, greenest thing in the world, it's called Ireland, the land of saints and scholars and poets. Now one of these Irish poets happened to be in Crampton tonight and he kind of sensed that here in this house was gathered a group of people who love poetry and would give him a warm welcome. He knocked at the door and walked straight in—just the way the wandering poets do in Ireland. His name is Michael Love—why the name is like a poem —he's a singer and he's just as Irish as can be. Mr. Michael Love, the Crampton Circle.

(She yanks him forward. He bows.)

THE PUPPETS. Ahhhh! *(and they eat ice-cream).*

MRS. BECK. Mr. Love is just longing to sing to you after he's shaken hands with you all, but before he does that I want to spring my last and my biggest surprise. Mrs. Swaffer's wonderful Union has given us many a treat but never such a wonderful one as this afternoon when we were addressed by the great English novelist Mr. Chesterfield Wragsdale. Some of you, like me, were privileged to be there—Mrs. Hoffmann, I saw you there—but this Circle never I am sure

expected to see Mr. Wragsdale in our midst
however the unexpected has happened and Mr.
Wragsdale is here, right behind me as I speak.

THE PUPPETS. Mmmmm!

MRS. BECK. I'm going to introduce you to
him now, and then he's promised to say a few
words to us. Mr. Chesterfield Wragsdale, the
Crampton Circle.

> (*She yanks him forward. He bows.*)

THE PUPPETS. Mmmmm!

MRS. BECK. Now before he gives us his message I want each one of you to meet him and I
want you to meet Mr. Love at the same time—
you've already had the pleasure of shaking
hands with Miss Waters. Mr. Wragsdale, will
you stand right here? (*She places him on the
extreme right of the opening and herself beside him.*)
You there, Mr. Love. (*She has him on the
other side of her.*) Now, Gordon, you stand
beyond Mr. Love and make the presentations.

GORDON. Yes, darling.

> (*He takes his place. The four are now in line
> in the order from left to right of* GORDON,
> MICHAEL, MRS. BECK, WRAGSDALE.)

MRS. BECK. Now friends, line up. Maybe
those at the left of the room would come
first.

VIVIENNE. May I slip out to the other room
and listen to the Negroes?

MRS. BECK. Certainly. (VIVIENNE *goes out.*)
Why, here's Mrs. Hoffmann, the very first.

(*A procession of puppets begins to move in procession from left to right. The puppets are exact replicas of the types who still stand in the room—the old, the middle-aged, the woman of twenty-three, and the girl of eighteen. Each puppet has its right arm extended. As the puppet reaches* GORDON *he names it.*)

GORDON. Mrs. Hoffmann, Mr. Love.

PUPPET HOFFMANN (*in artificial puppet voice*). Pleased to meet you, Mr. Love, I had an Irish grandmother.

MICHAEL (*shaking the hand*). How do you do?

(*The puppet passes on to* MRS. BECK.)

MRS. BECK. Mrs. Hoffmann, Mr. Wragsdale.

PUPPET HOFFMANN. Pleased to meet you, Mr. Wragsdale, I have read your books.

MR. WRAGSDALE (*shaking the hand*). How do you do?

(PUPPET HOFFMANN *passes out of sight on the right. By the time* PUPPET HOFFMANN *has reached* WRAGSDALE *another puppet— the middle-aged one—is being introduced to* MICHAEL *by* GORDON. *Everyone says exactly what has been said on the occasion of* PUPPET HOFFMANN'S *introduction. The middle-aged is followed by the woman of twenty-three, then comes the girl, then another old woman. Except that the name varies with each puppet the procedure repeats itself till the end of the act. The whole thing grows more mechanical, the living people grow mechanical, like puppets themselves. Perhaps a gramophone reiterating names of women, " How do you do, pleased to meet you, I had an Irish grandmother, how do you do, pleased to meet you, I have read your books," will give the best effect. Through it all is heard the music in the distance of a Negro spiritual. The light in the room grows strange and artificial— odd. It fades from the front of the stage, except in one place where on the English settle* BIRDIE *and* CARL *are sitting. They are quite human and natural.)*

CARL. It's crazy, just plumb crazy.

BIRDIE. Line up and meet Europe, Carl.

CARL. Not for me.

BIRDIE. Silly!

CARL. I'm right, I know I'm right.

BIRDIE. You're just dumb.

CARL (*his arms round her*). America's good enough for me.

BIRDIE. Look out, they'll see.

CARL. Not a chance of it. Their eyes are glued on Europe.

BIRDIE. We seem kind of left out of it.

CARL. As long as they keep on forgetting us. Say, Bird, will you marry me right away?

BIRDIE. Right away?

CARL. I want you, Bird. You don't know how much I want you.

BIRDIE. I like you too, Carl, and maybe next year after I've been to——

CARL (*putting his hand on her mouth*). Don't say the word.

BIRDIE. But next year——

CARL. Next year nothing. Next week. To-morrow. Oh, Bird, say you will.

BIRDIE. All right, Carl.

CARL. When?

BIRDIE. Any old time.

CARL. That means tomorrow.

BIRDIE. Not quite literally.

CARL. Amendment accepted. And Europe's cut out?

BIRDIE. Yeah.

CARL. Now and for always?

BIRDIE. Now and for always.

CARL. Sign here, along the dotted line. (*He kisses her.*) We'll be just Americans?

BIRDIE. Yeah, just Americans.

CARL. No truck with Europe?

BIRDIE. Not a bit.

CARL. Sign again. (*He kisses her.*) And our kids, they'll be American? A hundred per cent. little Americans?

BIRDIE. You bet. (*And without waiting to be asked she signs again.*)

CURTAIN.

ACT III

Four weeks later. A private dining-room in a superior speak-easy in New York. The room is decorated in very quiet, very good taste. Formerly it was the inner drawing-room of one of New York's fashionable houses and the double doors leading to the large drawing-room have been removed and the space filled with glass panels draped with heavy curtains. This space is in the centre of the stage at the back, and through the glass we can see from time to time dancing couples, and we hear, very faintly, a jazz orchestra. The dancers conform closely to one or two types, all the men are dressed in "tuxedos," and though the colour of the girls' dresses varies, they do not vary in cut, nor in the way the hair is dressed. The couples dance slowly, without animation; they are not puppets, but they approach them as nearly as human beings can. When the characters on the stage join in the dancing, they, too, become puppet-like.

*There is a large round table in the middle of the room and two waiters—*HENRI *the head-waiter and an under-waiter called* ED.*—are putting the last touches to their preparations for*

a supper for six people. On the wall at the
back is a bracket and on the bracket a radio
loud-speaker.)

HENRI (*speaking with a marked French accent*).
We need now only the glasses and the serviettes.
Fetch them, Ed. Hasten yourself. Monsieur
Brice said ten o'clock and it is now that hour.

ED. (*speaking in a strong New York accent*).
Sure. Champagne glasses?

HENRI. I do not know. Monsieur Brice
he did not order the wine. You do better to
bring ordinary glasses and the glasses for the
champagne.

ED. Sure.

    (*He goes out. Henri continues for a minute*
      to prepare the table. Then NICHOLAS
      BRICE *and* WRAGSDALE *come in, both are*
      wearing dinner jackets.)

NICHOLAS. Bonsoir, Henri. (*He speaks fairly*
good French with a bad accent.)

HENRI. Bonsoir, Monsieur Brice.

NICHOLAS. Mr. Wragsdale, this is Henri
Leprevost, the best waiter in New York and a
cultivated Frenchman into the bargain.

WRAGSDALE. Good-evening.

HENRI. Good-evening, sir. I think that
Monsieur Brice flatters me.

NICHOLAS. Vous avez mis pour six?

HENRI. Oui, Monsieur, six couverts.

NICHOLAS. Et tout est prêt?

HENRI. Tout est prêt, Monsieur, tout à fait

prêt ; sauf le vin que vous n'avez pas encore commandé.

NICHOLAS. Nous voulons commencer par cinq Baccardi cocktails.

HENRI. Cinq seulement, Monsieur?

NICHOLAS (*reproachfully*). Henri!

HENRI. Oh pardon, Monsieur. J'oubliais que Monsieur ne prend jamais de cocktail.

NICHOLAS. Alors, je pense, un Bourgogne. Avez-vous encore de Pommard, cet Pommard qui *était* un Pommard?

HENRI. Oui, Monsieur. Je me suis entendu avec le patron pour vous réserver tout ce qui restait. Il y a encore six bouteilles.

NICHOLAS. Merci.

HENRI. Pardonnez-moi, Monsieur, mais êtes-vous bien sûr que vous ne désirez pas un peu de soupe pour commencer?

NICHOLAS. Poulet mayonnaise, asperges nature, bombe glacée——— What do you say, Wragsdale?

WRAGSDALE (*who has taken no interest in this conversation, because he has not understood a word of it, starts to attention at his name.*) Eh, what? What do you want?

NICHOLAS. Shall you feel starved if you have only chicken mayonnaise, asparagus and an ice? Henri seems to think it's a mean supper.

WRAGSDALE. Plenty for me. I never take much supper.

NICHOLAS. I thought that as in two hours' time you'll be facing the Atlantic——

WRAGSDALE. Exactly.

NICHOLAS. Alors, ce sera bien ainsi, Henri.

HENRI. Bon, Monsieur. (*To* ED. *who is now back with glasses and napkins.*) Do not trouble about the champagne glasses, they will not be required. (*They place the other glasses and the napkins on the table and go out.*)

WRAGSDALE. That makes me very envious.

NICHOLAS. What?

WRAGSDALE. Your gabbling away in French.

NICHOLAS (*very vain of it but pretending modesty*). Oh, I've plenty of words but not much of an accent I'm afraid. You speak it surely?

WRAGSDALE. Just enough to ask my way and what time the train leaves. I never could manage the lingo.

NICHOLAS. I can't imagine going to France and not speaking the language—or indeed going to any country without speaking its language.

WRAGSDALE. English carries you everywhere.

NICHOLAS. Not quite everywhere I think.

WRAGSDALE. Everywhere that matters. As you're going to live in Spain I suppose you speak fluent Spanish.

NICHOLAS. Pretty good.

WRAGSDALE. It seems to me extraordinary— your choosing Spain.

NICHOLAS. Why extraordinary?

WRAGSDALE. I can of course understand a cultivated American like you feeling that he can no longer bear to live in the States, but (*he hesitates*)——

NICHOLAS. You would have expected me to choose England ?

WRAGSDALE. That makes me sound conceited. Shall we say the British Isles ?

NICHOLAS. I prefer my old Spanish town.

WRAGSDALE (*a trifle pugnaciously*). Why ?

NICHOLAS. So many reasons. I think I shall say " climate " and leave it at that.

WRAGSDALE. The English climate is the best in the world. Charles the Second said there were more days in the year on which a man could be out of doors in England than in any other country—and remember, Charles knew Spain.

NICHOLAS. Well then it can't be climate, I must think of something else.

WRAGSDALE. For shooting and hunting——

NICHOLAS. But I neither shoot nor hunt.

WRAGSDALE. Abroad is all right for a holiday, but to live there——! When do you leave ?

NICHOLAS. I think another couple of months will see everything wound up.

> (MOLLY O'SULLIVAN *comes in. She is dressed in charming taste quite simply and inexpensively. She has the right sort of hat, the right shoes and stockings, powder on her face but no lipstick. She has a*

*hundred per cent. more assurance than in
Act One and quite a considerable amount
of New York accent.)*

MOLLY. Mr. Brice, am I too late or too
early ?

NICHOLAS (*shaking hands*). Neither, Molly,
just right.   Here's Mr. Wragsdale.

MOLLY (*shaking hands with him*). How do
you do ?   You're sailing tonight ?

WRAGSDALE. Yes.

MOLLY. I'm glad I'm not. Gee, such a
wind !   It sent me spinning.

WRAGSDALE. I remember you're not a good
sailor, fortunately I am, never was sea-sick in
my life.

MOLLY. I hope to goodness Michael'll be
sick—he's so conceited about himself.   Send
me a postal if he is, Mr. Wragsdale, promise.

WRAGSDALE. When are you coming back
yourself ?

MOLLY. Not for ages.   I've got to work and
make money.

WRAGSDALE. I thought you only came out to
fetch your nephews back to Ireland.

MOLLY. Yes, but when I laid eyes on them
I knew they'd never do a day's good in Killeen.
They're just two little New Yorkers, and so
smart, and the education they're getting, and
their religion is looked after well—no, I knew
I'd be doing the worst thing by them to cart
them back to Ireland.

WRAGSDALE. And it seems to me that you're rapidly becoming a New Yorker yourself.

MOLLY. Well you see I had to stay on for a bit till my brother's affairs were settled up, Mr. Brice helped me about that.   Mr. Brice is surely one of the kindest people I've ever met.

NICHOLAS. Now, Molly !

MOLLY. You needn't listen if you don't want to but you can't stop me telling everyone how kind you've been to me.   He got me a job in a shop—one of those small special shops you know, not a big department store—and I'm working hard and learning the business and doing a course of typing and shorthand in my spare time, and I'm earning enough to live in a little room all by myself and soon I'll be able to put by money to bring my aunt out to live with me——

WRAGSDALE. At her age?

MOLLY. Oh she's not so old, and we're not like the English, Mr. Wragsdale, New York's a sort of second home to the Irish.

WRAGSDALE. You're here for good and all then?

MOLLY. I suppose so.   I'd like to go back in a way, sometimes I get very lonesome for the country, but I wonder could I ever stick it now.

NICHOLAS. Sometimes, Molly, I feel a little guilty to think that it was I who made it easy for you to stay.

MOLLY. Ah, give over !   Ireland will get on

very well without me. And look what I've got for you, Mr. Brice. A little medal my aunt sent you, it was blessed by the Pope. I've told her every letter how good you've been to me and she told me she started praying for your conversion so I told her that you were a better Catholic than herself and of course that delighted her out and out and nothing would do her but that you should have the medal. Will you wear it?

NICHOLAS (*taking it*). Of course. You must give me her address, I must write and thank her.

MOLLY. That'll delight her. Ah, here's me bold Michael!

(MICHAEL *comes in, he is dressed in a dark suit.*)

MICHAEL. Hallo, Molly. How do you do, Mr. Brice? Good-evening, Mr. Wragsdale. Look, Mr. Brice, I've done an awful thing, I wonder will you be mad with me. I ran up against two friends of mine in the street, they've just been married and they're off to Europe for the honeymoon—they're sailing on our ship. Before I knew what I was saying I asked them to supper and bundled them into a taxi and drove here. Then I remembered it wasn't my supper——

NICHOLAS. That's quite all right. Where are they?

MICHAEL. Downstairs. I told them to wait below. You're sure you don't mind?

NICHOLAS. Quite certain.   Bring them up at once.

MICHAEL. Thanks very much. (*He goes out.*)

MOLLY. Well, I give Michael ten for coolness.

NICHOLAS. It's rather characteristic of the way you Irish cling together out here, Michael can't resist an Irish face and I declare I don't blame him.   Thanks to Miss O'Sullivan, Wragsdale, I've grown very fond of the Irish colony here.   (*He rings a bell.*)

MOLLY (*laughing*). You should see him at a *ceidhl*, Mr. Wragsdale.

WRAGSDALE. What's that?

MOLLY. Oh, an Irish party.   Singing and dancing you know. . . . Say, may I have a cigarette while we're waiting for Michael's Irish butties?   I'm parched for a smoke.

WRAGSDALE (*offering his case*). Here you are.

MOLLY. Mr. Brice doesn't like girls smoking, but all Irish girls smoke.   That was one of the few things New York didn't have to teach me. (*She lights up.*)   I'm just blind ignorant, Mr. Wragsdale, but I'm learning fast, amn't I, Mr. Brice.?

NICHOLAS. You certainly are, Molly.

MOLLY. You won't know me when you get back from Spain.

NICHOLAS. You seem mighty certain I'm coming back.

MOLLY. Sure you'll come back. You couldn't live the rest of your days in a slow old country like that.

WRAGSDALE. That's what I've been telling him.

MOLLY. I give him three months, end of that time Spain won't see him for dust.

(MICHAEL *comes in with* BIRDIE *and* CARL. CARL *looks worried in a too-new suit.* BIRDIE *is bursting with the assurance of the young married woman.*)

MICHAEL. Mr. Brice, meet my friends Mr. and Mrs. Svenson.

NICHOLAS (*shaking hands with* BIRDIE). How do you do? I'm very glad to meet any of Mr. Love's Irish friends.

BIRDIE. I guess I can't claim to be very Irish, 'cept for my grandmother, she was from those parts. It's very very sweet of you to let us crash in on your party tonight.

NICHOLAS. Not at all. How do you do, Mr. Svenson?

CARL. Pleased to meet you, Mr. Brice.

MICHAEL. And this is Miss O'Sullivan.

BIRDIE (*shaking hands*). Pleased to meet you, Miss O'Sullivan. You sound like the genuine Celtic article.

MOLLY. How do you do?

BIRDIE. This is my husband. He's pretty raw as a husband—only two days old.

MOLLY. How do you do?

CARL. Pleased to meet you, Miss O'Sullivan.

MICHAEL. I believe you know Mr. Wragsdale.

BIRDIE. Why, if it isn't Chesterfield Wragsdale. Well I say! (*She shakes hands.*) We never knew we were going to see you here tonight.

WRAGSDALE. How do you do? So glad to see you again.

BIRDIE. This is my husband. I can't remember did you meet him that night at Mrs. Beck's. Yeah, of course you did, he was razzing Europe.

WRAGSDALE (*with a slight grin*). He was. How do you do?

CARL (*conscious that the laugh is on him*). Howdy.

WRAGSDALE. You're going there all the same?

CARL. Yeah.

WRAGSDALE. Congratulations.

CARL. Thanks.

> (HENRI *appears with a tray of cocktails.*)

NICHOLAS. Merci. Mettez deux autres places aussi vite que possible. Posez les cocktails, nous nous servirons nous-même.

HENRI. A l'instant, Monsieur. (*He puts the tray on the table and goes out.*)

NICHOLAS. Will you all help yourselves?

> (*They help themselves and the party divides,*)

WRAGSDALE *and* BIRDIE *find themselves together*.)

WRAGSDALE. So you're going to Europe after all?

BIRDIE. After all? What d'you mean?

WRAGSDALE. I seem to remember that your husband had a slight prejudice against Europe.

BIRDIE. Oh, that was only hot air. You see my uncle gave us a wedding present, a return ticket to Europe for the two of us and a thousand dollars in travellers' cheques. Wasn't that a dandy present?

WRAGSDALE. Delightful.

BIRDIE. So we're making a quick trip, only six weeks altogether, Carl can't leave the farm for long. Maybe I'll stay behind in Europe for a bit, maybe I'll wait on for the Becks and spend the summer with them.

WRAGSDALE. It's a little early in the year for Europe.

BIRDIE. We're aiming at Africa, we're going to Algiers.

WRAGSDALE. I see. Softening your husband's fall.

BIRDIE (*with a secure smile*). I guess I'll yank Carl across the Mediterrean before I'm through.

WRAGSDALE. I expect you will.

(HENRI *and* ED. *appear with extra supper things and rapidly lay two more places*.)

NICHOLAS. I want to tell you all—Mr. Salmon is supping with us tonight. His play closed about six weeks ago, he hasn't been very successful I'm afraid so we'll all be a little extra nice to him and won't ask him too much about his experiences in the States.

MICHAEL. Surely. But where's Miss Waters, shouldn't she be here?

NICHOLAS. She'll be a little late, she had an engagement to sing over the radio. A cousin of yours got it for her I think.

MICHAEL. Tim Murphy. I know.

NICHOLAS (*looking at his watch*). She said not to wait supper for her. She ought to be on just about now. Henri, faites marcher le radio s'il vous plait.

HENRI. Certainement, Monsieur. (*He switches it on.*)

ANNOUNCER'S VOICE. ——reacted sharply at mid-day on fresh selling of merchandise issues and utilities, varied by a small flurry of buying in copper issues. The market closed irregular. Call money lower by one half per cent. The day's sales totalled 3,197,000 shares. This concludes the stock-exchange news. . . . This is Station WXYZ broadcasting from the Wilson Tower. You will now hear Miss Vivienne Waters who is brought to you through the courtesy of the Peak Motor Car Company of Crampton, manufacturers of the famous Peak touring car and also of the little run-about popularly called the Peek-a-boo——

BIRDIE. Do you hear, Carl?

CARL. Sure I hear. Good old Peak!

ANNOUNCER. Miss Vivienne Waters is better known as the Old Rose of Wild England and she——

VIVIENNE'S VOICE (*in agonised protest*). No, no, the Wild Rose of Old——

ANNOUNCER (*to* VIVIENNE). What? Oh, of course. (*To the public.*) I beg her pardon, Miss Waters reminds me that she's the *Wild* Rose of *Old* England. Miss Waters is right at the top of the tree as a singer of English tunes and I know you'll appreciate her. She's anxious to say a few words to you before she starts in to sing.

VIVIENNE'S VOICE. Good-evening, friends. I feel so shy at having to speak to you over the radio—the wireless as we call it in England. I am sure I would not feel so shy if I could see your faces for I am sure I would find friends among them, I have made so many friends during the months I have spent in your great big beautiful country. I sail home tonight but I look forward so much to coming back here in the autumn—the fall as you call it—and my next visit will be a long one. Now my speciality is English folk-songs but I also sing Scotch and Irish ones——

MICHAEL. You do!

VIVIENNE. And tonight I am just going to give you one of each, but in compliment to America and in thanks for all its kindness I am going to begin with one of your own beautiful songs.

MICHAEL. What's she going to put over? " The Star-spangled Banner?"

WRAGSDALE. Ssh!

> (*A piano is heard playing a prelude, then* VIVIENNE *starts to sing.*)

MICHAEL (*after half a minute of it, with a roar of laughter*). Well I'm blest! I wouldn't put it past her. She's pinched the Niggers' songs.

> (*It is indeed one of the spirituals we heard in Act Two.*)

NICHOLAS. A spiritual? I can't bear them. Henri, arrêtez le radio, s'il vous plait.

HENRI, Certainement, Monsieur.

> (*He does so. By this time the table is arranged and he and* ED. *are about to go.*)

NICHOLAS. Nous allons commencer maintenant, nous n'attendons pas l'autre monsieur. (EDWIN SALMON *appears.*) Ah, here he is. (HENRI *and* ED. *go out.*)

NICHOLAS (*shaking hands*). How do you do, Mr. Salmon, I am so glad you were able to come. I think you know everyone here—oh no, of course—Mrs. Svenson, Mr. Salmon, and Mr. Svenson.

BIRDIE. Pleased to meet you, Mr. Salmon.

CARL. Howdy.

EDWIN. How do you do?   How do you do, Wragsdale?

WRAGSDALE (*shaking hands*).   Glad to see you again.

MICHAEL. Hallo.   How's the form?

EDWIN. Rotten, thanks.   You sailing tonight too?

MICHAEL. Yes.

EDWIN. Lucky dog.

MOLLY. I believe you've forgotten me.

EDWIN. I—I—you're—— ?

MOLLY. Molly O'Sullivan, on the boat, do you remember?

EDWIN. Of course.   Bally stupid of me.

MOLLY. I'm not surprised you didn't recognise me.   That black dress I had!   I made a bonfire of it before I was here a fortnight.

EDWIN. You're also shaking the dust tonight?

MOLLY. No, I'm staying on.

EDWIN. Hard luck.

(HENRI *and* ED. *are back with the chicken mayonnaise.*)

NICHOLAS. Will you all sit down?   I want Miss Molly on one side of me and I'll keep the other side vacant for Miss Waters.

MICHAEL. I'm going other side of Molly, the Irish must stick together.   And maybe Mrs. Svenson will help to look after me.

BIRDIE. I guess you need some looking after.

NICHOLAS. Wragsdale, perhaps you'd sit the

other side of Miss Waters' chair with Mr.
Svenson beside you and then Mr. Salmon—yes,
that's right.

> (*They all sit down, there is half a minute's
> silence, the waiters are serving.*)

BIRDIE. I don't know, Mr. Salmon, that any
of us are to be congratulated on sailing tonight.
I thought our taxi would be blown over on Fifth
Avenue.   I reckon this is the last square meal
I'll eat in days.   You feeling scared, Carl?

CARL. No.

BIRDIE. Isn't he the big brave strong man?
Imagine, he's never seen salt water in his life.

EDWIN (*with his usual gloom*). I'd face a
hurricane, I'd face thunder and lightning, I'd
face ice-bergs to get away from New York
tonight.

BIRDIE. Say, what's New York been doing to
you?

EDWIN. It's done me in, it's done me brown.

NICHOLAS. Cheer up, Mr. Salmon.   You're
sailing in six or seven days aren't you?

EDWIN. I hope so.

WRAGSDALE. What boat?

EDWIN. An awful tub called the *Circe*.

WRAGSDALE. What line is that?

EDWIN. The   Amalgamated   International
Steamship Company.

WRAGSDALE. I don't think I ever heard of it.

EDWIN. I don't think anyone ever did—
except me.

NICHOLAS. How long do they take to make the passage?

EDWIN. I don't know, no one knows. I don't believe they ever get to the other side, I don't believe they're ever heard of again after they leave America.

CARL. What makes you choose such a bum line?

EDWIN. It's cheap. If you can tell me a cheaper I'll go by it.

NICHOLAS. We're all sorry you haven't been luckier. I'm afraid you got into a bad play.

EDWIN. I don't mind the play failing—any play may do that, though it was a dashed good play, above the heads of the people here, that's why it failed. But they kept me here for six weeks after I landed before they put it on and when it came off after less than three weeks' run of course I couldn't get another job thanks to your precious Equity.

NICHOLAS. Yes, it's a bit hard on you.

EDWIN. Then I try to get into the speakies, they *say* they want cultivated English voices, but don't you believe it, I've tried and I know.

CARL. I guess you won't ever come back to the States again.

EDWIN. Not if I can help it.

CARL. Why can't we all stick to our own country?

EDWIN. Of course it's jolly easy to understand

why Americans want to come to England, people like yourself for instance——

CARL. I don't want to come, my wife's dragging me, and anyway we're not going near England. No, sir.

BIRDIE. Cut that out, Carl. He's really so excited about coming, Mr. Salmon. Say, have any of you ever been to Algiers?

EDWIN. No.

NICHOLAS. I have. Why?

BIRDIE. Isn't it true that you can get the most wonderful carpets there just for a few dollars?

CARL. Now, Bird Svenson, are you thinking of going into competition with Mrs. Beck and making an oriental corner out on the farm?

BIRDIE. Of course not. But we must have a few rugs laying around, and if I can pick them up cheap—and those sort of tables with brass trays on them, they're cute I think, and a few——

CARL. Go on, go on. She'll end by turning the place into a harem.

BIRDIE. Just you wait, Carl Svenson, you'll be so proud of your home. There won't be another like it, not for three hundred miles.

NICHOLAS. Remember, Mrs. Svenson, there are such things as United States Customs.

BIRDIE. I'll remember. I've been in Europe before and I'll say that our officials don't let much by.

EDWIN (*very aggrieved*). They tried to make me pay income tax. I didn't know people like me ever did pay income tax.

NICHOLAS. Don't you pay in England?

EDWIN. Never. They'd never have the nerve to ask me. I suppose some people do.

WRAGSDALE. I certainly do. I look on it as a social duty.

EDWIN. Oh, you can afford it, I can't. And that's why I think it's so dashed hard to try to grab my hard-earned dollars.

NICHOLAS. How about you, Mr. Love, did you have to pay?

MICHAEL. I got off lightly. You see I've a sort of cousin in the business so he wasn't hard on me. I lectured to his Club for nothing. But don't let's talk of nasty things like taxes. What about a dance to liven us up, eh, Molly?

MOLLY. I don't think so, Michael. I've not got into the way of dancing in the middle of eating.

MICHAEL. Any time's a good time for a dance. What about you, Mrs. Svenson?

BIRDIE. I'd love it.

MICHAEL. Good. And look, there are three girls at a table in the next room, they're with a sort of cousin of mine, they'd love a dance I know. What about it, Carl? And Salmon and Mr. Wragsdale?

CARL. I'm on.

EDWIN. I don't particularly want to, but I don't mind.

WRAGSDALE. I'm afraid I don't know them.

MICHAEL. But I do. One of them's a great reader, always stuck in a book but quite pretty. If you dance with her she'll boast of it all her life.

WRAGSDALE. Well, really——

MICHAEL. Come along, be a sport. You're sailing in a couple of hours, you can't seriously compromise yourself in that time. You don't mind Mr. Brice, do you, if we have a turn? There's nothing to get cold. You don't dance yourself I think?

NICHOLAS. No. Run along.

MICHAEL. Come on so.

(*They all go out except* NICHOLAS *and* MOLLY.)

NICHOLAS. You're sure you don't want to dance?

MOLLY. Certain. I'm feeling a bit down tonight.

NICHOLAS. I'm afraid my little supper isn't going to be a great success. Mr. Salmon is a distinct damper and I don't know that I like those young Americans.

MOLLY. I don't think you're very gone on anything American.

NICHOLAS. I don't think I am.

MOLLY. It seems queer not to like your own country.

NICHOLAS. I don't believe I ever had any

feeling for America except as a place to make money in quickly and get out of as often as possible.

MOLLY. I think if I was an American I'd be very proud of the States.

NICHOLAS. My mother loved Europe, she dragged me across Europe when I was nine years old. You've seen those dreadful American brats who poison hotels abroad ?—well, I was one of them, but less brattish than most. The very first trip I went—we were in Italy, in Bologna I think—I said to my mother "Let's stay here always, don't let's ever go back to nasty America." Not bad that from a kid of nine.

MOLLY. It was horrid. If a child of mine said that to me about Ireland I'd beat it. . . . I wish you weren't going.

NICHOLAS. Why, Molly ? Why do you wish that ?

MOLLY. I'll be terribly lonesome when you've gone.

NICHOLAS. Will you ? Ah no, you've made so many friends in New York.

MOLLY. There's none of them like you. You've been so good to me and I'm sure I don't know why.

NICHOLAS. Why shouldn't I do what I can for you ? . . . I suppose I seem very old to you?

MOLLY. No, not so terribly old. My aunt's older.

NICHOLAS. I'm really only forty-eight, I know I look more like sixty, that's because I work so hard for eight months of the year to earn four months' holiday. You won't know me after a year of Europe.

MOLLY. You'll be like an old horse that's put out on grass.

NICHOLAS. Something like that, I suppose.

MOLLY. But if you're never coming back I'll never see how young you look, I'll never see you again. Oh, doesn't that sound awful? Ah sure, give up the idea, Mr. Brice.

NICHOLAS. Awful? Does it really sound awful to you? It does to me—never seeing you again I mean. That's why I was wondering . . . whether you wouldn't come with me.

MOLLY. Go with you? To Spain? And what would I be doing in Spain?

NICHOLAS. I mean come with me as my wife.

MOLLY. Oh, Mr. Brice!

NICHOLAS. I know I'm many years older than you but that needn't prevent a very happy marriage. I love you very dearly, we're both Catholics, I've plenty of money——

MOLLY. Please, please, Mr. Brice.

NICHOLAS. Couldn't you think of me as a husband, Molly?

MOLLY. I'm so sorry, I never dreamt——

NICHOLAS. I won't let you say "no" now, think it over. You've trusted me with all your affairs since you came to New York and I don't think they've turned out too badly. Can't you trust me with yourself for the rest of your life?

MOLLY. I couldn't, Mr. Brice, indeed I couldn't. Such an idea never entered into my head. Of course I knew you liked me—but to want me as a wife! And sure I must stay on here and work and save money to bring me aunt out——

NICHOLAS. Can't you understand that I have enough money for forty aunts? You need never work again.

MOLLY. But that was what was so lovely, working here and being independent. If I married you all that would be over.

NICHOLAS. I'd give you all the independence you want. If you cared for me——

(*The waiter* ED. *comes in.*)

ED. You're wanted on the phone, Mr. Brice.

NICHOLAS. Oh. . . . Excuse me just a minute.

(*He goes out followed by* ED. *There is a minute's pause, then* MICHAEL *comes in.*)

MICHAEL. I wish you'd come and dance, Molly.

MOLLY. I don't feel like dancing. What's happened your partner?

MICHAEL. She met someone she knew, a girl from her home-town, she's talking to her. Where's Mr. Brice gone to?

MOLLY. He's telephoning.

MICHAEL. His sort is always telephoning.
. . . (*He sits down, there is a short silence.*)
What's up, Molly?   Is something after happening?

MOLLY. Yes, Michael.

MICHAEL. What is it?

MOLLY. Mr. Brice wants me to marry him.

MICHAEL. That old codger!

MOLLY. He's not a codger, and he's not so
old—only about forty.

MICHAEL. Sure that's all ages.

MOLLY. I suppose it is.

MICHAEL. Did you give him the go-by?

MOLLY. I did.

MICHAEL. Good girl.

MOLLY. I'm wondering was I right.   After
all, he's awfully nice and he's been a good
friend to me.   I'd never have got the better of
Julia only for him.

MICHAEL. Of course you were right.   He's
O.K. but he's terribly romantical.   His grah
for Europe and all that.

MOLLY. Yes, he's romantical right enough,
but sure all Yanks are.

MICHAEL. You're right, Molly, they are.
Do you know, since I've come out here I feel
as hard as nails.   I sit around as cold as the
Cross of Cong and they romance about their
money, their country, their wives, their children,
the number of motor cars per head, the number
of their millionaires who live to be ninety, the

number of millionaires that die at twenty-five. Damn it all, there isn't a thing they won't get a wet eye about; it's all the same to them, Ireland's struggle for freedom or Italy's struggle for servitude, they've a sympathetic tear for each. I sit around just numb, and I wonder am I the only sensible man in the company or am I just a young heartless fool.

MOLLY. Just a fool.

MICHAEL. Maybe. But I'd rather be foolish the hard way than the soft way. . . . I'm glad you didn't link yourself up with a Yank.

MOLLY. I like him awfully. He's been as good as gold to me but I couldn't see myself married to him.

MICHAEL. Of course you couldn't. Yet in a way, Molly, I suppose you haven't much sense. Nicholas Brice has thousands and millions of dollars. He's a " warm man " as we say at home.

MOLLY. I suppose he is.

MICHAEL. Yes, you are a bit of a fool. As foolish as myself, legging it back to Ireland when I ought to stay here and marry you.

MOLLY. If I'd have you.

MICHAEL. If you'd have me, as you say. But the sensible thing for you to do would be to have me——

MOLLY. If you'd ask me.

MICHAEL. Exactly. If I'd ask you.

MOLLY. But you won't.

MICHAEL. And you wouldn't have me if I did.

MOLLY. I wouldn't.

MICHAEL. So there we are.

MOLLY. There we are. Cho mí-ghradhmhar le Eirennach.

MICHAEL. What does that mean?

MOLLY. The old Scottish saying : "As loveless as an Irishman."

MICHAEL. I'm not, Molly, I'm not. But we're too young to settle down.

MOLLY. You'll never settle down, Michael Love.

MICHAEL. I don't feel I ever will. I'm wild to be off tonight and no sooner will I have set foot in Ireland than I'm sure I'll be wild to be back here. That's the kind I am. Sure even in Ireland I was always hither and thither, I had my old father bothered.

MOLLY. You're a bird-alone.

MICHAEL. There's some itch on us Irish, we can't be content. Even in Paradise we'll be trying to shape it to the image of Cork.

MOLLY. You're just a fool, Michael Love.

MICHAEL. I know I am. . . . You'll write to me, won't you?

MOLLY. Maybe.

MICHAEL. And I suppose you'll marry some smart Yankee, damn him.

MOLLY. Maybe.

MICHAEL. Remember, I loved you first.

MOLLY. A queer sort of love.

MICHAEL. Give me a fortnight's notice of your marriage and I'll cross the ocean, race him to the altar and beat him.

MOLLY. I wonder.

MICHAEL. I will. I swear I will.

MOLLY. You can go marry any girl you like, it won't knock a feather out of me.

MICHAEL. Is that the truth? Is that the truth, Molly O'Sullivan?

MOLLY (*getting up, she is on the verge of tears*). Oh, go and dance. I'm sick of you and your talk. Ah, here are the others, thank God.

(BIRDIE, WRAGSDALE *and* CARL *come back and sit down and go on with supper.*)

MICHAEL. Where's our bold actor?

WRAGSDALE. He stopped behind to talk with your friends. Where is Mr. Brice?

MICHAEL. Telephoning.

CARL. That actor man is telling your friends all his troubles. He sure is sore about America.

MICHAEL (*to* WRAGSDALE). How did you hit it off with the young lady?

WRAGSDALE. She was charming, very intelligent.

MICHAEL. Had she read your books?

WRAGSDALE. Er—— I believe she had.

MICHAEL. What did I tell you?

BIRDIE. This will be a red-letter evening in her life. Say, Mr. Wragsdale, you must let me dance with you before the evening is over, I can't let that girl get away with it alone, I'm not going to let her be unique.

WRAGSDALE. I shall be delighted—though I'm afraid I'm not a very good dancer.

BIRDIE. It's not your steps, it's your—your——

CARL. Atmosphere.

BIRDIE. That's the word, Carl. Atmosphere.

(NICHOLAS *comes back, followed by* HENRI *and* ED. *who change plates and serve asparagus.*)

NICHOLAS. Forgive me for leaving you—a stupid telephone call. What was the dancing like?

BIRDIE. Fine, the room's a bit small but the band is good.

MICHAEL. I know the fellow who plays first fiddle.

BIRDIE. I suppose he's a "sort of cousin" of yours?

MICHAEL. Well, as a matter of fact, he is. I can't help it, America's plastered with my relations.

VIVIENNE (*putting her head round the door*). Have you eaten everything?

NICHOLAS (*rising, as do all the men*). Why, Miss Waters! Weren't you quick?

VIVIENNE. Wasn't I? I had a taxi waiting and I hopped into it the minute I was through and got here in no time. How do you do, everyone? I'm not going to shake hands with anyone except Miss O'Sullivan because I haven't seen her for an age. (*She shakes hands with her, then sees* BIRDIE *and* CARL.) Oh . . . now I have met you both . . . quite lately. . . .

BIRDIE. Crampton. Carl and I are partners now—life-partners. We're going to Europe with you tonight.

VIVIENNE. How wonderful!

NICHOLAS. Will you sit here? There's chicken mayonnaise. Henri!

VIVIENNE. No chicken, thanks. May I just have some of that delicious-looking asparagus? I'm not really a bad sailor but there's a wind tonight that does make me a little nervous.

NICHOLAS. Sure? Very well. (HENRI *serves her with asparagus.*) A cocktail to start with?

VIVIENNE. No thanks, just a very little wine. (*He serves her.*) Thanks.

BIRDIE. I'm sure you're dry after all that singing.

VIVIENNE. Oh, it was only for a few minutes, but I felt so shy and nervous.

MICHAEL. Yes, we heard your shyness.

VIVIENNE. You don't mean to say you were listening?

MICHAEL. Till Mr. Brice froze you out, he won't stand for nigger stuff, too American for him.

VIVIENNE. How awful of you to listen. If I'd known!

CARL. It sounded swell. (EDWIN *comes back.*)

137

EDWIN. How do you do, Miss Waters? You passed the table I was at and you cut me dead.

VIVIENNE. I didn't mean to. I'm so sorry.

MICHAEL. How did you get on?

EDWIN. Only so-so.

CARL. I suppose you told them what a rotten deal you got here in the States?

EDWIN. Yes.

CARL. Were they sympathetic?

EDWIN. No.

BIRDIE. What a shame.

EDWIN. I don't think Americans *are* very sympathetic.

NICHOLAS. Miss Molly, you're eating nothing and you're saying nothing.

MOLLY. I'm all right, Mr. Brice, only I don't much care about asparagus.

NICHOLAS. Then go right on to the ice.

MOLLY. I don't want any ice.

NICHOLAS. What can I get for you?

MOLLY. Nothing.

MICHAEL. Cheer up, Molly.

MOLLY. I was just thinking—Mr. Brice, doesn't this remind you of something?

NICHOLAS. No. I don't know what you mean.

MOLLY. All of us here together. Doesn't it remind you of the morning on the ship the day before we landed in New York?

NICHOLAS. Yes, of course.

MICHAEL (*to* BIRDIE). We all sang songs, we had a regular concert.

MOLLY. You're all going off—for even you'll be gone soon, Mr. Brice—only me will be left. I'm suddenly feeling awfully lonely.

MICHAEL. Buck up, Molly, we'll be back in no time, I will anyway.

MOLLY. It won't be the same thing somehow, never again. This is like the end of a bit of life. I'd love to end it with a song.

NICHOLAS. Why not?

BIRDIE. Say, wouldn't it be lovely to have Miss O'Sullivan sing?

MOLLY. No, no, I don't want to sing but I feel I'd love to hear a bit of music.

NICHOLAS. Miss Molly must be obeyed. Who shall start? Mrs. Svenson?

BIRDIE. I can't sing. A little tinkle on the piano is all I'm good for.

NICHOLAS. Well, Mr. Love. We know you can.

MOLLY. Not Michael first, Mr. Brice. I'd like to sort of end up with Michael.

CARL (*with determination*). I can sing.

BIRDIE. You certainly can not.

CARL. That's all you know about it.

BIRDIE. Bunk.

CARL. Maybe you never heard me but I sing sure enough.

MICHAEL. Good man, start away!

CARL. I can't sing without a banjo or a ukelele.

BIRDIE. Oh, that sort of song! Carl Svenson, have sense.

MICHAEL. I'll get one for you in a trice. The leader of the orchestra's a sort of cousin of mine. (*He jumps up and goes out of the room.*)

BIRDIE. I warn you all I'm not responsible for Carl, I'm only married to him two days.

VIVIENNE. What sort of songs do you sing?

CARL. Cowboy stuff.

BIRDIE. What did I tell you?

VIVIENNE. That sounds interesting.

CARL. Of course I was never West myself but I had a bunch of cowboys working for me a couple of summers ago and I picked up some of their songs. Maybe you won't like them, they're pretty simple.

BIRDIE. I should say they were. They're just crude.

CARL. They're American. Michael tells me, Mr. Brice, that you're quitting America, that you don't think much of us. Maybe you'd rather not hear an American song.

MOLLY. Oh please say you want to hear one, Mr. Brice.

NICHOLAS. Of course I do. I hope I'm not as prejudiced against America as all that.

BIRDIE. You will be when you've heard cowboy songs. For the land's sake, Carl, lay off singing.

CARL. Not on your life.

(MICHAEL *is back with a guitar.*)

MICHAEL. They wouldn't give me the uke so I pinched a guitar.

CARL. That'll do fine. (*He starts to tune up.*) You'll have to excuse me, I'm only an amateur.

(*At reasonable intervals the waiters change plates and serve the ice, and then coffee and liqueurs.*)

CARL (*singing simply and excellently*).

" O bury me not on the lone prairie,"
These words came low and mournfully
From the pallid lips of a youth who lay
On his dying bed at the close of day.

He had wailed in pain till o'er his brow
The shades of death were gathering now,
And he thought of home and his loved ones
    nigh,
While the cowboys gathered to see him die.

" Oh bury me not on the lone prairie,
Where the wild cyotes will howl o'er me,
In a narrow grave just six by three,
O bury me not on the lone prairie."

" It matters not, so I've oft been told,
Where the body lies when the heart is cold,
But grant, O grant, this prayer to me,
And bury me not on the lone prairie."

And the cowboys now as they ride the plain,
For they marked the spot where his bones were
    lain,
Fling a bunch of roses upon his grave,
With a prayer to Him Who his soul will
    save.

VIVIENNE. You'll have to teach me that on
the boat. Will you?

CARL. Sure.

MICHAEL. Your autumn tour?

VIVIENNE (*with a twang*).   Sure!

NICHOLAS. Now Miss Molly, if you won't
have Michael next you'll have to fill the gap
yourself.

MOLLY. You know what a poor singer I am.

NICHOLAS. On the contrary, I remember you
sang charmingly.

MOLLY. What'll I sing, Michael?

MICHAEL. Anything at all, but let it be jolly.
None of those dreary old things about Croppy
Boys and the like.

MOLLY. Somehow I can't think of anything
very gay.

NICHOLAS. Sing whatever you feel inclined to.

MOLLY. There's an old song my mother
used to sing—'tis only an old country song, it
keeps running in my head tonight, I don't
know why.

NICHOLAS. Let's hear it please.

MOLLY. I think I half-forget the words.

Maybe I'll remember it as I go on.   Here it is anyway.   (*She sings.*)

" Oh, I'll not sit on the grass," she said,
   " Nor be a love of thine,
For I hear you love a Connacht maid,
   And your heart is no longer mine," she said,
   " And your heart is no longer mine."

" Oh, I'll not heed what an old man says
   Whose days are well-nigh done.
And I'll not heed what a young man says,
   For he's fair to many a one," she says,
   " For he's fair to many a one."

"Oh, I will climb a high, high tree
   And rob a wild bird's nest,
And back I'll bring whatever I do find
   To the arms that I love best," she said,
   " To the arms that I love best."

(*She sings the song with such intensity that there is an awkward silence when she finishes, then a conventional murmur of applause from all except* NICHOLAS *and* MICHAEL. NICHOLAS *is really moved and she suddenly realizes this.*)

MOLLY (*turning to him and taking his hand and stroking it*). Mr. Brice, I didn't think—I didn't mean—it just came into my head—that old song——

NICHOLAS. All right, Molly, all right.

143

MICHAEL (*rather loudly*). Well then I can beat you, Molly O'Sullivan, for melancholy and broken hearts. Hear you are. (*Singing.*)

> Down by the salley gardens my love and I did meet ;
> She passed the salley gardens with little snow-white feet.
> She bid me take life easy, as the grass grows on the weirs ;
> But I was young and foolish, and now am full of tears.

(*Waiting for no applause.*) Oh, to the devil with this melancholy! If we go on like this, next thing we'll be doing is putting back our heads and howling like dogs.

> (*He sings at tremendous speed and with great verve.*)

> Beauing, belling, dancing, drinking,
> Breaking windows, damning, sinking,
> Ever raking, never thinking,
>   Live the rakes of Mallow.

> Spending faster than it comes,
> Beating waiters, bailiffs, duns,
> Bacchus' true-begotten sons,
>   Live the rakes of Mallow.

> Racking tenants, stewards teasing,
> Swiftly spending, slowly raising,
> Wishing to spend all their lives in
>   Raking as in Mallow.

Then to end this raking life,
They get sober, take a wife,
Ever after live in strife,
    And wish again for Mallow.

    (*The song comes as a blessed relief to the
       whole party, there is general applause
       and a request for another.*)
No, no, that's enough songs for the present.
Come on and dance. Molly O'Sullivan, I dare
you to stand up on the floor with me.

    MOLLY. I'm not afraid of you, Michael
Love. (*She stands up.*)

    MICHAEL. Good girl! I must take back the
instrument. (*They go out, he carrying the guitar.*)

    BIRDIE. Mr. Wragsdale, your promise.

    WRAGSDALE. Certainly. (*They get up.*)

    EDWIN. Miss Waters, are you too tired?

    VIVIENNE. No. But have we time?

    NICHOLAS. You have time enough. I'll
stay and settle my bill.

    (*The three couples go out, leaving* NICHOLAS
       and CARL *and the waiters.*)

    NICHOLAS. Henri, l'addition, s'il vous plait.

    HENRI. Tout de suite, monsieur. (*He and*
ED. *go out.*)

    CARL (*after a silence*). Why are you quitting?

    NICHOLAS. Quitting? Oh, leaving America
you mean?

    CARL. You're not an old man, you've been
pretty successful I hear, why do you quit?

NICHOLAS. Just because I've been pretty successful and because I'm not an old man; there's time left for me to enjoy life.

CARL. What's the matter with life here, can't you enjoy it here?

NICHOLAS. No.

CARL. Why?

NICHOLAS. Too big and noisy and quick and new.

CARL. I know that's what Europeans say but they come from slow old places. You were born this side, weren't you?

NICHOLAS. Yes.

CARL. Then all our bigness and noise should come natural.

NICHOLAS. Somehow it's never come natural to me, the more I live in America, the more I hanker after Europe.

CARL. Won't you find it hard to start in over there?

NICHOLAS. Start in? What do you mean?

CARL. But maybe you're going into partnership with someone.

NICHOLAS. Oh . . . no, I'm not going to go on with my business.

CARL. Then what are you going to do?

NICHOLAS. Nothing—except enjoy myself.

CARL. *Nothing?* You mean that, honest?

NICHOLAS. Yes. I'm just going to enjoy life in my quiet, middle-aged way.

CARL. I see.

NICHOLAS. You mean you don't see. I shock you, I think. I shock most of my American friends. They don't hold with anyone who just idles, who's just out to enjoy life.

CARL. Life's not meant just to be enjoyed.

NICHOLAS. I'm hurting no one by going, I've very few relations and they're all independent of me.

CARL. You're hurting America.

NICHOLAS. I can't imagine how.

CARL. It's—I don't suppose I've got any right to say these things to you, Mr. Brice,—but seems to me it's kind of disloyal of you to quit. It makes out that America's not good enough for you.

NICHOLAS. It isn't. That's the whole truth of the matter. I'm European, all my tastes, all my thoughts are European ; every year I live here I see this country swinging west, turning in on itself. Every old book, every old master you buy stamps you as being non-European, you buy them as curiosities, as examples of a civilisation not your own. I want to live in a country where these things are taken for granted—so taken for granted that the country lets them go to America without a pang, with no sense of loss.

CARL. They're hollering about all we're taking.

NICHOLAS. They needn't. A few yards of canvas, a few pages of print—Europe will be

Europe without these things. And they won't make America less American, they're museum pieces, curiosities, nothing else. No, America's just not good enough for me.

CARL. You could hang on and help make it good enough.

NICHOLAS. I haven't that much faith in my own power—or in America.

CARL. I know we're blamed crude, some of us. I guess Crampton's a pretty crude place but I'm going to hang on there, I hope I don't ever leave it.

NICHOLAS. And you'll work and work and grow richer and richer?

CARL. I aim at that.

NICHOLAS. And will that help Crampton and America?

CARL. Sure.

NICHOLAS. That's just where we differ. I don't believe the States will be fit to live in till people like you are glutted with work and money, till you've made so many dollars you just get sick and start to idle. But that's for your son—or your son's son. It won't come in my time so I'm going to quit.

CARL. I'm going to Europe tonight and I'd make you a present of my ticket if I could.

NICHOLAS. I should like to meet you when you get back, maybe you'll have changed your mind.

CARL. You think I'll fall for Europe?
Birdie's half over the edge already.

NICHOLAS. I guess you're pretty safe, I
expect you'll remain faithful to Crampton

CARL. I hope to tell you!

NICHOLAS. But as you *are* going, take my
advice ; don't waste your time on Algiers, it's
vulgar, second-rate French. Get on to Tunisia,
see the old Greek and Roman stuff there, see
Carthage drowned in poppies and wild barley,
see back in the country those dead Roman
cities " By the caper over-rooted, by the gourd
over-scored."

CARL.

" While the patching houseleek's head of
        blossom winks
    Through the chinks—
Marks the basement whence a tower in
        ancient time
    Sprang sublime—— "
Good stuff, isn't it? And then that other
thing about " A rose-red city, half as old as
time."

NICHOLAS (*staring at him*). I say! Maybe
you're not as safe as I thought you were.

CARL. Maybe I'm not, that has me half-
scared. That's why I'd like to pass my ticket
on to you. I like poetry, I can't help liking
poetry. I'd like to write poetry about Crampton.

NICHOLAS. It's hardly inspiring, is it?

CARL. Yeah it is, for the right person. I've

tried but it don't come right, it's too much like second-rate English stuff. I guess the only poem I'll ever write will be the farm.

NICHOLAS. You're a farmer?

CARL. Yeah. God, I wish I was catching the midnight train back. I'd be there the morning after tomorrow and Mike'd meet me with the little Peak, and in two hours I'd be out there. We'll be ploughing soon, and the garden's sheltered, we get things real early there, Mr. Brice, little flowers and the shrubs breaking into leaf. I can't get used to the idea of being away from it, I can't get used to the idea of not working for weeks and weeks. I'll be nicking off the days till I get back—like a kid waiting for the holidays.

NICHOLAS. I talk of America—and I really only know New York State.

CARL. It's pretty out there in the summer when the corn's up—and there's a creek, I used to go fishing there when I was a kid. It's "bonny"—that's what an old Scotsman my dad used to have called it. "Bonny"—isn't that a nice word? Do you think Europe will make me blind to the—the bonniness of it?

NICHOLAS. I hope not. After all, Tunisia is a farmer's country.

CARL. Is that so? Do they farm there?

NICHOLAS. Certainly. Do you imagine they live on the ruins of Carthage? If you get scared of those rose-red cities, if you feel they're putting something over on you, go and inspect one of the big farms.

CARL. I certainly will. There's plenty I've got to learn about a farm. I want my farm to be the best farm for a thousand miles around. I won a bunch of prizes at the county show last year. Yes, sir. I thought when I got married I could settle down and give my whole mind to it and now first thing I know I'm hitting the trail for Africa.

NICHOLAS. How will your wife like living on a farm?

CARL. Remains to be seen. Bird married me with her eyes wide open. She's all right, only a bit Europe-sick. She's a notion of sticking there all summer, but no, sir, I won't stand for that. She sails home with me in six weeks' time.

(HENRI *is back with the bill.*)

HENRI (*presenting it*). Monsieur.

(NICHOLAS *examines it, takes out a couple of bills and gives them to* HENRI.)

HENRI. J'apporte la monnaie à l'instant, Monsieur.

NICHOLAS. Et j'ai besoin deux taxis.

HENRI. Parfaitement, monsieur. (*He goes out.*)

CARL. This is a nice joint. Say, it was kind of you to have Bird and me here tonight.

NICHOLAS. Will you look me up when you come back? I don't expect I'll have left—that

151

is unless you fall for Europe to the extent of staying there all the summer. (*He hands him a card.*)

CARL. No fear of that. Thanks, Mr. Brice, we surely won't pass through New York without ringing you up.

(*All the others come back from dancing.*)

VIVIENNE. And now, Mr. Brice, I really think we should be making a move. I've got to call at my hotel for a suit-case.

BIRDIE. So have we.

MICHAEL. I invite you all on board for a final drink. My bootlegger cousin in Chicago has fixed me up very nicely, thank you.

NICHOLAS. I'm just waiting for my change. My car is outside and I've ordered a couple of taxis. You'll come to the boat, Molly, won't you, and Mr. Salmon?

MOLLY. I'll come to be sure. I must see Michael safely off.

EDWIN. Thank you very much, I'll come only it'll make me so jealous, I'll probably cry myself to sleep.

(*The door opens.*)

NICHOLAS. Ah, here is Henri with my change.

(*But it is not HENRI. It is UDOLPHUS immaculate in full evening dress.*)

UDOLPHUS. Good-evening, ladies and gentlemen.

MICHAEL. Dolphy!

MOLLY.
VIVIENNE.
WRAGSDALE.
EDWIN.
} Udolphus !

UDOLPHUS. Pardon the intrusion. I saw you dancing and I made enquiries and found you were in here and on the point of leaving these hospitable shores, so I thought you'd forgive the liberty——

MICHAEL. Of course. But I say, Dolphy, you do look a swell.

UDOLPHUS (*very pleased with himself.*) Yes, sir. Best tailor in Liverpool, sir.

MICHAEL. May one ask why ? Come in for a fortune ? Left the ship ?

UDOLPHUS. Not at all, sir. But the Company, sir, have been kind enough to give me three months' leave.

WRAGSDALE. And you're going to make a trip through the States ?

UDOLPHUS. Yes, sir. A lecture-tour.

MICHAEL.
VIVIENNE.
WRAGSDALE.
{ What? Well, I'm damned.
A lecture-tour ?
Lecturing ?

UDOLPHUS (*beaming*). Yes sir, yes miss.

WRAGSDALE (*a little severely*). May I ask what you are lecturing on ?

UDOLPHUS. The title of my lecture, sir, is " Celebrities I have Served."

EDWIN. By Jove !

UDOLPHUS (*to* WRAGSDALE). I am using a

little anecdote about you, sir, I hope you will forgive the liberty, it is calculated not to give offence.

WRAGSDALE. And whom are you lecturing to?

UDOLPHUS. Only to the best Universities, sir, and to the ladies' clubs.

WRAGSDALE. Who is your agent?

UDOLPHUS. Mr. Koffmann, sir. He deals in you too, sir, I think.

(HENRI *is back with the change which he hands to* NICHOLAS.)

MICHAEL. Come on down to the boat, Dolphy, we're all going.

UDOLPHUS. Oh no, sir, I only dropped in to bid you good-evening.

MICHAEL. You must come, you can introduce us to the smoke-room steward and tell him we're nice people who must be allowed to run up bills. He must come, mustn't he, Miss Waters?

VIVIENNE. Certainly. Please, Udolphus.

UDOLPHUS. Very well, miss, if you say so. I shall be most happy.

VIVIENNE (*getting into her wrap*). And now for England, home and beauty.

BIRDIE. Our things are downstairs. Got the check, Carl?

CARL. Sure. (*He and* BIRDIE *go out.*)

EDWIN (*drifting out*). I believe I've lost my bally check.

VIVIENNE. Your coat and hat downstairs, Mr. Wragsdale?

WRAGSDALE. Yes, come along. (*They go out followed by* UDOLPHUS.)

    (NICHOLAS *is tipping* HENRI. *At the door* MICHAEL *and* MOLLY *find themselves together.*)

MICHAEL. Forgive and forget. Be a sport, Molly. Give me a kiss.

MOLLY. No. (*She goes out quickly.*)

MICHAEL (*pursuing her*). Wait till I get you on the boat!

HENRI (*pocketing the tip*). Merci, Monsieur Brice.

NICHOLAS. Bon soir, Henri. (*To* ED.) Good-night.

ED. 'Night.

    (NICHOLAS *goes out. The waiters start to clear up.*)

ED. Decent guy.

HENRI. Monsieur Brice? Yes. He think he can speak French!

ED. Well, can't he?

HENRI. He speak bum French. And the accent! Mon Dieu, very very bad.

ED. Same as your American.

HENRI. You say I not speak American?

ED. Not so as you'd recognise it. We're different, you see. Just blamed different.

HENRI. Different? In what way we are different?

ED. Take too long to tell you. I'm American, you're French. That's saying everything. Get me? Different? Yes, sir. And always will be.

THE END.

Ever the Twain was produced for the first time in the Abbey Theatre, Dublin, on October 8, 1929, with the following cast :

CHESTERFIELD WRAGSDALE	F. J. McCormick.
VIVIENNE WATERS ...	Meriel Moore.
EDWIN SALMON	Arthur Shields.
UDOLPHUS	P. J. Carolan.
NICHOLAS BRICE ...	Michael J. Dolan.
MICHAEL LOVE	Michael MacLiammoir.
MOLLY O'SULLIVAN ...	Frolie Mulhern.
MRS. GORDON A. BECK	Christine Hayden.
GORDON A. BECK ...	Eric Gorman.
BIRDIE CUMMINS ...	Eileen Crowe.
CARL SVENSON	Michael Scott.
FOUR NEGROES	W. J. Roderick Rafter, R. V. Rafter, C. L. Rafter, E. Russell Rafter.
HENRI	A. J. Leventhal.
ED.	Joseph Linnane.

The scenes for the first and second acts were designed and painted by D. Travers Smith. The play was produced by the author.

The verse and chorus of " She was just a Sailor's Sweetheart " are printed by kind permission of Messrs. Francis, Day and Hunter, Ltd.

PRINTED IN GREAT BRITAIN BY
BILLING AND SONS LIMITED,
GUILDFORD AND ESHER